canoe routes
yukon territory

Published by
The Mountaineers
719 Pike Street
Seattle, Wash. 98101

ISBN 0-91689060-0

Photographs by the authors unless otherwise credited.
Printed in Canada by Hemlock Printers Ltd.
Layout by Frebo Studio Limited

PRINTED IN CANADA
THE MOUNTAINEERS

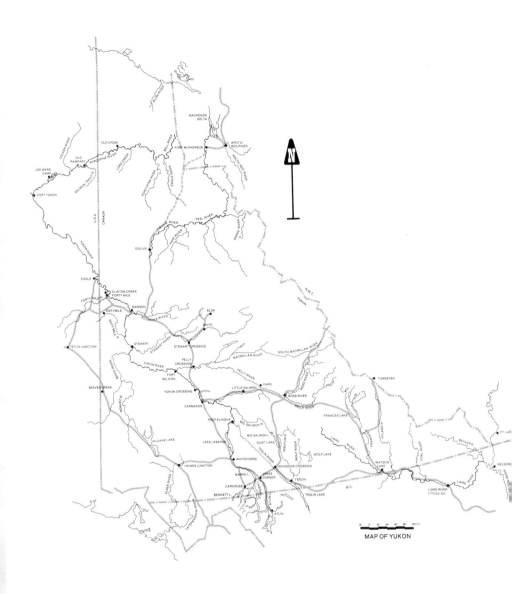

MAP OF YUKON

INDEX TO CANOE ROUTES OF THE YUKON TERRITORY

Grizzly Bear.

INTRODUCTION

The Yukon Territory is bordered and crossed by mountain ranges from which many great rivers are born. The word Yukon (Youcon) in fact comes from the Indian word which means big river or great river. Most of the territory was discovered, explored, mined and settled via its water routes, the main arteries of transportation until recent years.

Today canoeing is still an ideal way to explore the Yukon, to enjoy its rich history, magnificent scenery, abundant wildlife and wilderness adventure. Much of the land is still wilderness, though this is changing with increased interest in the Yukon's resources and as a route for Alaskan resources. To travel this country by canoe is to see it in its most natural form, providing the canoeist with a healthy form of recreation and an incomparable adventure, while keeping peace with the environment.

The geographic location of the Yukon produces conditions which limit the season during which its waterways are navigable, but which make that short period unique. There is almost around-the-clock daylight for example in June and July throughout the northern half of the Yukon. A combination of these long daylight hours, with the relatively high temperatures and moderate precipitation of the summer months produces phenomenol growth in plant life from what amounts to a twenty-four hour a day growing season. The rivers may be canoed between spring break-up in May until fall freeze-up in about October. However the best time for travel is from the middle of June until the end of August.

This publication is a where-to rather than a how-to book, for there are already many fine books available by experts on the techniques and skills required in canoeing. Many of these are listed in the Bibliography, but there are two books that we have found particularly helpful which we feel are worthy of special mention. Our own introduction to canoeing was Bill Riviere's *Pole, Paddle & Portage, A Complete Guide to Canoeing,* which is a good basic paddling book. For those who are into wilderness canoeing, a recent publication, *The Complete Wilderness Paddler* by James West Davidson and John Rugge, is both helpful and presented in an interesting manner. We also recommend that a basic paddling course by taken to facilitate learning some of the skills involved in canoeing.

The route information in this book does not tell the complete story of the water routes of the Yukon. Rather it is the putting into print and sharing with others the material and experiences that we have been able to compile up to the present time. The gathering process will continue for us and we hope that future editions of this publication will reflect additional research, including more of our own canoeing experiences on Yukon rivers. For now, this information is as complete and up-to-date as possible, but is not meant to be the only source of reference. For example detailed maps have purposely been excluded from the book since we feel that obtaining topo maps is critical to safety in navigating rivers and travelling in the wilderness. The maps included are simply to give a general idea of the courses of rivers, and of the position of lakes and rivers in relationship to the areas in which they are located. Additional suggestions of reading material relating to specific areas have been included within the route descriptions.

The limited details regarding flora, fauna, history and geology which are found in the route descriptions are included to whet the appetite; for we believe that part of the fun in travelling a route is in discovering things for oneself.

Along with the routes we have prepared a section on safety, since we feel a responsibility to those who we may be encouraging to get out onto the water. However we can only write these things down - it is up to the individual to arm himself or herself with the knowledge and equipment on which lives may depend.

The compiling and writing of this canoe trip guide and its companion volume, *Canoe Routes British Columbia,* was much more difficult than had been anticipated. Not for a lack of routes, or a lack of enthusiasm, but because during the whole course of the project our weathered 17 foot prospector Chestnut sat across two saw horses an arm's length from the typewriter. And it needed a lot of work. Last summer while on a journey across the prairies, a gale snapped the tie-downs and bounced it along the highway. Emergency repairs made it floatable, but it needed a few ribs, and planks patched and some rather extensive canvas repairs. It was often a test of will power to decide which was the most important, a book on canoe routes, or the canoe; and each time we researched a new journey it seemed to be more urgent to get those patches on. How can one write about the Porcupine or Pelly, or remember the Liard and northern lakes with a holed canoe close at hand? Even research seemed to steal time from actual writing. I mean you can't just read a *little* of Warburton Pike, and when friends are telling you their stories you have to add a few of your own. And how many trips and expeditions have we planned and practically canoed while writing? When could we take that trip? Harold wants to go back to the Yukon next summer - maybe he'll join us on the Teslin, and Jim wants to try the Bell-Porcupine, and Dave and Jan the Nisutlin. I wonder when the ice goes out on the Arctic Coastal Plain? Enough trips and friends to paddle for years - and most of them are recorded here. Now if we can just get that final coat of paint on .....

Richard Wright
Rochelle Wright
Port Moody, B.C.

HISTORY

The history of canoeing the Yukon is in many ways synonymous with the history and development of the Yukon Territory, for the native people, the fur traders and the gold seekers lived on, travelled by, worked in and settled along her rivers and waterways.

Evidence has been found proving that the Yukon area has been habited for at least 7000 years. Earlier migrations across the Bering Strait from Asia through Alaska and the Yukon to all parts of the Americas are believed to have begun as long as 20,000 years ago. The natives who made the Yukon their home used dugout canoes and skinboats to travel the rivers for their own use and for trading.

The discovery, exploration and mapping of the Yukon Territory was accomplished by a number of men of varied nationalities and interests. For example, the Russian traders, after establishing their sealing and otter industries, extended their explorations up the Yukon River as far as the Nowitna River. However it was the early Hudson's Bay Company explorers and fur traders who were the first to extensively travel the interior of the Yukon, naming most of the rivers. In 1840 Robert Campbell journeyed up the Liard into the Yukon discovering the Pelly River. Then in 1842 he returned to build Fort Frances, the first Hudson's Bay fur trading post within what is now the boundary of the Yukon Territory. The following year he descended the Pelly as far as the Lewes (Yukon) River. Far to the north in the years 1840-1844 John Bell established trading posts for the

Gold Nugget - The lure of the Klondike.

Miles Canyon on The Yukon.

H.B.C. at Fort McPherson on the Peel River and Lapierre House on the Bell. He also followed the Bell-Porcupine Rivers to where they joined what Bell heard the Indians call the Youcon River. Construction and exploration continued around the two known points on the Yukon River, with Robert Campbell naming most of the tributaries of the Yukon and eventually reaching Fort Yukon at the junction of the Pelly and Yukon in 1851, thereby connecting his own post and discoveries with those of other H.B.C. explorers.

Many problems beset the early traders. Posts came and went, and gradually the traders were joined by others who came to live and work in the Yukon - missionaries, miners, surveyors, government officials and the N.W.M.P. By the time the Klondike Gold Rush really began there were already more than 1000 gold miners working along the Yukon River and its tributaries. After the discovery of gold on Bonanza Creek in 1869 by George Washington Carmack, Skookum Jim and Tagish Charlie, word quickly spread, and more than 50,000 people headed by steamer, rail, foot and makeshift boats to the Klondike. Many lives were lost in the Miles Canyon area of the Yukon until the N.W.M.P. instituted strict controls and only allowed those boats through that had "sufficient freeboard" and were "steered by competent men."

After the search for furs and then for gold abated, the Yukon River continued to be the main transportation route until the completion of the Alaska Highway during the Second World War. Now a network of roads connects the major centres and rivers of the Yukon and searches continue for other sources of riches.

CLASSIFICATION OF RIVERS

The classification of rivers according to a standard can be valuable as a general guide to the navigability of the river. However all water bodies including rivers are living, moving, changing entities which vary with the weather and the seasons. It is difficult therefore to grade rivers without elaborating on all the possible variations and changes.

The recognized standard for the grading of rivers is the International River Classification. We have used this grading system for our routes, based on the most recent and accurate information that we could obtain.

This standard of classification does have some limitations which should be taken into consideration by the canoeist. The International Classification is based on easy access and egress and average water levels; it does not make allowances for loaded canoes and cold water. So in a wilderness situation, the dangers associated with a graded section of water may be increased where help is not readily available, and may make unrunnable that which could easily be done in a controlled situation. For example an experienced paddler who was normally capable of handling a Grade 3 rapid may only be able to cope with Grade 2 water with a loaded canoe, where cold water and difficult access make a spill too risky. Another limitation of this system is in the grading of large volume rivers where the volume provides a powerful force with boils and souse holes, which can be dangerous even within a Grade 1 section of water. The final consideration in classification is to understand that a rise or fall in the level of the river can alter the grade of a section of river within a very short period of time.

These are not new ideas we are presenting on the complexities of wilderness canoe travel. Here is what Warburton Pike wrote about a trip down the Pelly in 1887:

"Unless in the case of a perfectly straight piece of water, when you can form a pretty good opinion of the danger by standing up in the stern of the canoe, it is always well to put ashore, and take a look at what lies ahead, when travelling down an unknown stream, as you may find yourself at the brink of a cascade, or an utterly impassable rapid, when it is too late to make a landing. Don't listen to the valiant fool in the bow, who shouts: 'Oh, hell! we can run that!' just as you are shooting into the eddy; and if he tries to enforce his opinion by dragging the bow of the canoe out into the current, no experienced voyageur will blame you for clubbing him on the head with pole or paddle. He cannot know anything more about what is round the corner than you do, if he has never seen the place before.

"It is pleasant enough to play about in the rapids in a light canoe when civilization is close at hand and the loss caused by a capsize or collision with a rock can be easily replaced; but when the accident happens 500 miles from the nearest trading-post the possible result of a mistake is serious enough to make the most reckless steersman reflect a little before he plunges his canoe into the swirling waters. If anything goes wrong it is a case of total shipwreck, and the men who reach the bank in safety are really little better off than those who come to sudden grief among the rocks. Everything is gone. There are no matches that would light a fire to dry the soaking clothes; no axe to build a raft with; nothing to eat: no rifle, ammunition, or fish-hooks with which to kill game or fish that would provide a means of subsistence to a properly equipped party. The only means of progression is a misshapen ungovernable raft of drift timber bound together with willow twigs and turned loose down stream till it flies to pieces on the first rock, or drifts under an overhanging log-jam, each accident being likely to further reduce the number of the crew."

The International River Classification

The following interpretation of the International River Classification is made by Canoe Sport British Columbia.

Grade 1
Easy. Waves small and regular; passages clear; occasional sand banks and artificial difficulties like bridge piers. Suitable for novices in closed canoes, kayaks and open Canadians.

Grade 2
Quite easy. Rapids of medium difficulty; passages clear and wide. Occasional boulders in stream. Suitable for intermediate paddlers in closed canoes, kayaks and open Canadians.

Grade 3
Medium difficulty. Waves numerous, high, irregular. Rocks and narrow (clear) passages. Considerable experience in maneuvering required. Advance scouting usually needed. Canoes will ship water, and unless equipped with spray covers, will require frequent emptying. Kayaks must be equipped with spray covers. Suitable for experienced paddlers in closed canoes and kayaks, and expert paddlers in open Canadians.

Grade 4
Difficult. Long rapids, powerful irregular waves; dangerous rocks, boiling eddies; passages difficult to reconnoitre; advance scouting mandatory; powerful and precise maneuvering required. Spray decks mandatory. Suitable for expert closed canoes and kayaks only. Not suitable for open Canadian canoes.

Grade 5
Very difficult. Extremely demanding long and very violent rapids, following each other almost without interruption. River bed extremely obstructed; big drops; very steep gradient; advance scouting mandatory and usually difficult due to nature of terrain. Suitable for expert paddlers only in closed canoes and kayaks with specific white water training under expert leadership. Not suitable for open Canadian canoes.

Grade 6
Extraordinarily difficult. The difficulties of Grade 5 carried to extremes. Nearly impossible and very dangerous. Suitable for teams of expert paddlers only in closed boats at favourable water levels and after careful study, with fully trained and experienced rescue team in position. Not suitable for open Canadian canoes.

CANOEING SAFETY

There are two aspects of safety to be considered by the canoeist - safety involving the water itself and survival in a remote or wilderness situation. The following pages cover the basic safety considerations for canoeists including some general rules for water and wilderness safety, a discussion of equipment and some first aid measures. It is recommended that the individual continue his or her own research by doing further reading or perhaps taking a course on canoeing or survival. Suggestions for supplementary readings are contained in the bibliography.

Early Day Canoeing.

Safety and Survival

Preparing oneself for a safe canoeing outing involves being well trained, knowledgeable and adequately equipped for the trip to be undertaken. The following are recognized rules for outdoor safety which relate to the canoeing experience

— Never canoe alone; for any trip into back country or a wilderness area, there should be a minimum of three canoes.
— Wear a life jacket, which has been tested.
— Learn paddling skills in a controlled situation.
— Know your own abilities and limitations.
— Be in good physical condition before attempting a long or difficult trip.
— Leave word with a responsible person indicating where you are going to canoe and when you expect to return; report back to them on your return. The R.C.M.P. request that all wilderness travellers obtain a Wilderness Travel Permit from them and fill in a form indicating departure date, route, and estimated time of arrival at destination. (R.C.M.P. detachments in the Yukon are listed in Appendix 5.)
— Carry emergency supplies, including extra food, change of clothing, canoe repair kit, first aid kit and survival equipment. (More details on emergency supplies are included in the section on equipment.)
— Watch for changes in the weather, and always be prepared for wind and rain.
— In case of sudden bad weather, find shelter.

- Keep dry and warm and watch each other for signs of fatigue or hypothermia. (More information on this condition is included in the section on hypothermia.)
- Be aware of changes in the river level causing rivers to be more swift and hazardous.
- Scout unfamiliar rivers by land in advance and note any hazards such as rapids, rocks, gravel bars, deadheads, sweepers or log jams.
- Go through rapids or hazardous spots one canoe at a time, allowing each one room to maneuver and putting only one boat at a time into a vulnerable position.
- Travel close to shore on lakes or on large rivers.
- Be aware of currents.
- Know and practice rescue techniques.
- In case of a spill: stay with the canoe, unless your life is endangered by rapids ahead or by the cold water; assist other canoeists where possible; hang onto the upstream end of the canoe to keep it between you and any hazards; try to swim the canoe to shore.

Priorities of Survival

In the event of making a decision to stay put and wait for rescue or wait out a storm, it is important to understand the priorities necessary to survival:

1. State of mind
2. Air
3. Shelter
4. Water
5. Food

The will to live and to think rationally through a problem without panicking gives a person the best possible chance of surviving any situation. The conservation of energy should be a key factor in making decisions. For example, swimming a long distance to shore is likely to be more of any energy drain than staying with a boat and gradually drifting and swimming it to shore; and searching for edible plants for food may use up more calories than it supplies.

As well as making provision for survival, use every effort to attract attention. Three fires are the recognized international distress code, so try building three signal fires. They should be 30 metres apart in a triangular formation, or where along a river bank or ravine, they can be in a line. The fires should be built in an open area as much as possible and should be protected from rain. They need not burn continuously, but can be lit at

intervals to attract the attention of anyone in the area, and should also be lit when aircraft are sighted. Smoke and fire together are effective around the clock.

Leader Responsibilities

Whenever a group of people are out canoeing together there should be someone who is designated as the leader to carry out the following responsibilities:
— Have good prior knowledge of the route to be canoed.
— Ascertain that the trip to be undertaken is not beyond the capability of any participant.
— Have preknowledge of medical problems and allergies of every member of the group.
— Be sure that each member is suitably clothed and equipped.
— Have knowledge of local weather conditions and probable changes in water levels.
— Proceed at the speed of the slowest participant.
— Keep the group together.
— Be willing to stop or turn back in case of hazardous weather or other problems.
— Monitor the physical conditions of members of the group.
— Make decisions relating to safety.
— Supervise rescue operations.

Equipment

The discussion of equipment here will primarily take the form of a list of gear to be considered for canoe outings, with a few comments, notes and hints included.

First though, here are some suggestions regarding the choosing of a canoe outfit. There is no best choice for any one person or any one situation. Individual preferences will vary according to the kind of canoeing to be done, the ruggedness and durability required in a canoe, finances, and personal taste. The basic equipment required is a canoe, paddles, and life jackets.

Since there are many variables it is wise to research what is available and what will best suit your requirements. Suggestions of ways to begin this research are:
— Read what the experts have to say about choosing equipment; several books in the bibliography include this kind of information.
— Talk to experienced canoeists; if you don't know any personally, check with a canoe club.
— Check out a minimum of two stores - if you deal with someone who is a canoeist, you are likely to get more knowledgeable assistance; avoid peak busy times to get the most help.
— Try renting different types of equipment; however it may be difficult to rent some things, such as a wood and canvas canoe (which requires more upkeep).
— Take a canoe course - canoes are usually provided giving the participant an opportunity to try out equipment with the added advantage of being able to obtain advice from the instructor.

Accoutrements to be considered when choosing a canoe include a keel, a bracket which will hold an outboard motor, a sail, and a pole, Also you will need a roof rack or some method of transporting the canoe.

Care of the canoe and its accessories takes some time and effort but pays off with fewer problems on the water, and longer service over the years. A few hints on protection, storage and maintenance follow:

— Fasten the canoe well while transporting it; having watched our own canoe blow off the van in a heavy wind and bounce down the road behind, we feel constrained to remind others to not only tie the canoe down well, but to also check the ropes and ties frequently.
— Avoid dragging over rocks or gravel bars.
— Have canoe parallel to shore and properly afloat while being loaded.
— Step into the water to board and leave a canoe at the water's edge, as wet feet are preferable to a scraped bottom.
— Swish each foot in water to rinse off sand and gravel when stepping into the boat.
— Lift canoe onto shore for overnight stops or if there are large waves.
— Store protected from extremes of weather - rain, snow, hot sun - preferably indoors; canoes can be suspended with ropes or on a rack; wood and canvas should not be turned upside down on the ground for any length of time unless set on boards, as dry rot is likely to set in where the canoe touches the ground.
— Store paddles by hanging or suspending to prevent warping.
— Store life jackets in a dry airy place.
— Maintain equipment in good order; keep surfaces well sanded and painted or varnished.

Basic Equipment

— Canoe - wood and canvas, fibreglass and aluminum are the main canoe types used in this area; should be tested before embarking on a long trip.
— Bow and stern lines or painters - should be attached to both ends of the canoe, rolled up neatly, but quickly available when needed; a floating type line 30-50 mm by a minimum of 5 metres is recommended (up to 30 metres may be required for lining or tracking a canoe).
— Spray covers - frequently used on open canoes in white water to keep waves out; are also useful in protecting gear in rainy weather, and to keep warmth in and wind out in cold weather.
— Paddles - one for each paddler plus a spare tied in but readily available for use.
— Life jackets - one for each person in the canoe; test while fully clothed - must be capable of supporting an unconscious person in face up position; should be worn at all times in a boat by children and non-swimmers, and should be worn by everyone whenever there is a chance of an upset.
— Knee pads - may be needed for comfort; never use life jackets to kneel on.
— Map and compass - important to know how to use.
— Matches in waterproof container (35 mm film cans are watertight) or firestarter.

- Knife - axe or saw may also be included.
- Shelter material.
- Food, utensils and cleaning items.
- Stove and fuel - not always necessary but advisable in parks or on longer trips where there may be some fire restrictions.
- Clothing suitable to the season.
- Change of clothing.
- Rain gear.
- Toilet articles.
- Toilet paper.
- Sun glasses.
- Sun protection cream.
- Lip ointment.
- Insect repellent.
- Mosquito headnets.

Nahanni Butte from Turner's Field.

First Aid Kit (in waterproof container)
- Butterfly tapes, gauze pads, tape, elastoplast bandage, tensors, slings, scissors, tweezers, safety pins, needle, antiseptic, vaseline, thermometer, salt tablets, pain medication, antiallergenic medication, personal medications, snake bite kit, calamine or zinc oxide lotion.

Canoe Repair Kit
- For wood and canvas tears this should include canvas patches and plastic resin marine glue; structural repairs are more complicated but can usually be improvised using a knife and sticks or wood available in the vicinity.
- Fiberglass repair kits should include fibreglass patching material and epoxy.
- Aluminum is less likely to require patching but more difficult to repair; temporary patching may be attempted with roofing cement or with a cloth patch glued with pitch or cement.

Survival Kit
- In addition to the basic equipment already mentioned, the following should be put into a compact watertight container and fastened to the belt of each canoeist.

— Map and compass, matches, knife, paper, pencil, signalling mirror, whistle, space blanket, snare wire, fishing kit, tinfoil (for cooking), emergency food rations eg. bouillon cubes, soup, tea, sugar, chocolate, salt.

Equipment for Overnight or longer trips
— Sleeping bags, ensolite foam pads for insulation, tent or tarp.

For carrying equipment in canoes, a few large packs are better than a lot of small containers; this is especially appreciated when loading and unloading the canoe, and when carrying over a portage. Ammunition boxes with rubber gaskets come in a variety of sizes and make ideal water-tight containers for cameras and film, first aid kits and repair kits. Heavy plastic laundry bags can be used to protect sleeping bag rolls.

Clothing

Clothing for canoeing should be chosen for comfort and safety rather than fashion. It should keep the individual dry and warm or cool and protected from the sun. As a general guideline clothing should provide good insulation, allow moisture to evaporate, be light, adaptable to changes in the weather or activity, and allow freedom of movement.

The system of dressing to best suit the above requirements is called layering. This involves wearing several layers of lightweight clothing which can be removed or added to keep warm or cool. Each layer serves to trap air and body heat. Wool clothing is recommended when it is cold, as wool retains insulating quality when wet to a much greater degree than any other kind of fabric. And wet clothes increase susceptibility to hypothermia due to heat loss. Layered clothing can be easily removed to prevent sweating and quickly donned when taking a rest or if a wind comes up.

The following clothing should be considered for canoeing excursions:
— Underclothing - wool recommended for chilly weather.
— Pants - wool or cotton, depending on the nature of the trip; jeans and tight pants should be avoided.
— Shirts - lightweight; long-sleeved in insect and sun country; also wool shirts for cooler weather and evenings.
— Jacket - should be windproof and lightweight; fibrefill retains insulating qualities even when wet.
— Socks - protect against cold feet and insects.
— Shoes - lightweight leather, moccasins or sneakers best in canoe; boots may also be wanted for portaging and camping.
— Hat - important for protection from wet, cold, sun and insects; up to 60% of body heat can be lost through an uncovered head.
— Gloves - may be needed on long paddles or in insect country.
— Rain suit - for keeping dry in the canoe and in camp.
— Rubber wetsuit - ideal in very cold water.
— Wetsuit socks - worth considering where there is considerable lining or tracking to do with wet feet.
— Complete change of dry clothes.

Food and Nutrition

Food is the fuel which provides the energy on which our bodies run. We require food to keep us warm and to supply energy for muscular work. Since canoeing can be a strenuous activity, caloric intake must be increased to provide energy for the physical exertion and to replace any heat loss from exposure to cold weather or water. Inadequate food intake combined with hard physical activity may cause food exhaustion, characterized by weakness, dizziness and nausea. It also makes a person more susceptible to hypothermia.

To maintain good nutrition while canoeing you should begin and end the day's activities with a substantial meal. Through the day it is best to eat frequent small meals and snacks. The powdered, dehydrated, freeze-dried foods available today are ideal to take along due to their light weight. However many of these tend to be expensive and some are of questionable palatability. Usually expense can be minimized by shopping at a large supermarket for such items as dried fruits, dried vegetables, instant rice, instant potatoes, packaged soups, powdered beverages, powdered desserts, nuts and seasonings. Packaging foods in meal-size portions in heavy plastic bags simplifies meal preparations in the outdoors. Fresh meat and vegetables can be used for the first day or two of any trip. Keep in mind too, that one of the advantages of canoeing is that you can handle more weight than with backpacking. The trick is to use the heaviest foods prior to any portages.

A word of caution for those travelling in bear country, which includes most of the Yukon: Food should never be left lying around camp or in tents. Pack it well and suspend it in a tree well away from camp. All food wastes should be burned.

Dehydration can be a problem, especially with heavy physical activity and in hot weather. Canoeists usually have little problem finding a water supply but should be sure that it is safe to drink. Contaminated water may be treated by boiling or with chemicals to render it potable. Replacement of electrolytes such as salt is equally as important as replacing fluids and can be accomplished by taking salt tablets. Inadequate replacement of fluids and salt results in a condition of heat exhaustion, with symptoms of thirst, weakness, faintness, nausea and cold clammy skin. Treatment includes rest, and a good intake of fluids and salt tablets.

Hypothermia

Hypothermia is a condition of the body in which the innercore temperature falls to a level at which the vital organs no longer function effectively. It is caused by situations in which the body loses heat faster than it produces heat. Hypothermia, known to many people as exposure, is a serious condition which will result in death if it is not recognized and treated in its earlier stages.

Normal body temperature is the result of a balance between heat production and heat loss. The primary sources of heat production are food and muscular activity, which are supplemented by external sources of heat

Wooden Frame for a Skin Boat.

such as the sun, a warm environment or the oral intake of hot fluids. Equilibrium of body heat is maintained by the cooling effects of radiation, conduction, convection and by the effects of evaporation, respiration and wind.

The specific factors which lead to hypothermia in the outdoors are cold, wetness, wind and fatigue. Since it is not uncommon for a canoeist to be confronted by a combination of these conditions it is vitally important that all canoeists be able to recognize the symptoms of hypothermia and be prepared to implement prevention and treatment. It is surprising to note that most hypothermia accidents occur between -1 and 10° Celsius (30-50°F).

Symptoms of hypothermia are easily recognizable to anyone who is aware of them. Everyone will already be familiar with the early stage of hypothermia characterized by feeling cold, feeling numb and shivering. As the state of hypothermia increases the following progression of symptoms will be noted:

1. Uncontrollable shivering.
2. Continued violent shivering, vague slow slurred speech, memory lapses and incoherence.
3. Muscular rigidity, fumbling hands, frequent stumbling, lurching gait, impaired judgement and reasoning power.
4. Drowsiness, apparent exhaustion and inability to get moving after a rest, irrational behaviour, drifts into stupor, decreased pulse and respiration rate.
5. Unconsciousness, reflexes cease to function, erratic pulse.
6. Failure of cardiac and respiratory centres in brain resulting in death.

Old Mine Car.

Prevention of hypothermia and its lethal sequence of symptoms begins at home with good preparations for the outdoors, and relies on alert responses to combat any problems that arise on an outing. Home preparation should include provisions for adequate rescue, clothing, shelter and emergency rations as well as a knowledge of the symptoms of hypothermia. Measures to avoid exposure include the following:

1. Dress appropriately.
2. Stay warm and dry.
   — Remove clothing before it gets wet from perspiration.
   — Put on extra clothing before you start shivering.
   — Put on rain gear before you get wet.
   — If you fall in the water, get into dry clothes and warm up before proceeding.
3. Keep rested
   — Travel at a reasonable speed.
   — Plan rest stops.
4. Maintain energy.
   — Eat nutritious meals
   — Nibble on snack foods such as nuts, dried fruit, jerky and candy between meals.
5. Be alert for signs of fatigue or symptoms of hypothermia in any member of the group.
6. Terminate exposure if you can't stay warm and dry in existing conditions.
   — Give up goal.
   — Seek shelter.
   — Build fire.
   — Camp or bivouac.

It is the nature of hypothermia that when an individual is no longer generating heat by himself, it is impossible for that person to rewarm himself; any application of heat must be provided by external sources. When progressive symptoms of hypothermia are recognized, exposure must be terminated and the following treatment begun immediately, even though the victim may deny that he needs help:

1. Get the victim out of the wind, rain and cold by providing shelter.
2. Strip off all wet clothes.
3. If mildly impaired, put into dry clothes and prewarmed sleeping bag; give warm, non-alcoholic drinks and candy or other sweetened food. If semi-conscious or worse, leave stripped and put in pre-warmed sleeping bag with another person, also stripped, or in a double bag between two stripped donors; must be kept awake and given warm drinks as long as conscious.
4. Use a thermometer to determine the extent of hypothermia and to measure recovery.
5. Build a fire to warm the camp.
6. When the victim has recovered sufficiently, feed him.
7. Make sure the victim is kept warm and dry on the trip out.
8. Get medical help. It is imperative that anyone who has suffered from the effects of hypothermia be taken for a medical checkup as soon as possible, even though the victim seems completely recovered.

General First Aid

In addition to hypothermia, there are a few other situations requiring minor first aid which may be of particular interest to canoeists, such as sun stroke, burns and insect bites. First though it should be stressed that all users of the outdoors should invest some time in a comprehensive first aid course. The importance of this kind of knowledge in a wilderness situation is obvious, but can also be useful when canoeing where help is nearby. For example the methods of applying artificial respiration may be needed at any time, and are best learned when they can be demonstrated and practiced under supervision.

There are, too, a few general precautions to be considered. Always carry identification, including important medical information; special medic alert bracelets can be purchased and engraved with this information. A good first aid kit is invaluable but it is of equal importance to know how to use it. The best first aid kit is one built on your own knowledge and designed for your own specific use; it should include medications and equipment to cope with personal conditions such as allergies.

In case of an accident, there is an order in which symptoms should be evaluated and treatment begun:
1. Keep calm.
2. Check respirations and give mouth to mouth artificial respiration, if breathing has stopped.
3. Check for bleeding and apply pressure to arrest it.
4. Check for injuries to head, neck and spine and for fractures or dislocations.
5. Treat shock, which is present to some degree in any case of injury.
6. Decide whether the victim may be taken to medical help, then proceed to evacuate; or send for help and provide shelter, food and care while waiting for assistance.

If someone is hurt and it is necessary to send for help, at least one person should stay with the injured party while one goes for assistance; if the group is large it is best to send two people. It is also important when sending for help in a medical emergency to write down as much as possible, such as the location, details of the extent of the injury, the name of the victim and the emergency contact at home. Where a rescue party is required, the R.C.M.P. will make the decision as to how the search and rescue is to be carried out.

Sunstroke
This is a condition which occurs when the body becomes overheated through exposure to the sun. The circulatory system has to work very hard to try and cool the body which results in a hot, flushed face, rapid pulse, weakness, dizziness and headache. Wearing a hat is the best prevention for sunstroke. Treatment includes rest out of the sun, drinking cold fluids, and a sponge with cool water. Sunstroke is not as obvious as the name implies and companions should be watched for symptoms.

Burns
Sunburns occur very readily in a water environment, and minor burns from a campfire or hot water are other possibilities on a canoe outing. Prevention of sunburn involves gradual exposure to the sun using a sun cream; after desired period of exposure, wear long sleeved shirt, long pants and a wide brimmed hat. In case of a minor burn from any cause, keep the

Black Bear.

burned area clean, out of the sun, and apply a soothing cream to keep the skin from drying. If the burn is serious enough to cause a blister or broken skin, cover the area with a sterile dressing and seek medical attention. Also take salt tablets and drink lots of fluids.

Wasp and Bee Stings

Unless an individual has developed an allergy to wasp and bee stings, the symptoms are usually fairly local ones - pain and swelling. Treat by removing the stinger, if there is one, and applying cold. Zinc oxide or calamine lotion may relieve any itching. An antiallergenic medication should be given for any sign of systemic involvement such as rapid pulse, shortness of breath or extensive redness and swelling. Anyone with an allergy to insect stings should have medical advice and carry medication with them at all times during the wasp and bee season. Once a person has had an allergic reaction, subsequent bites are likely to cause increasingly severe reactions.

Travelling in Bear Country

Since bears may be found almost anywhere in the Yukon, a wilderness traveller should always be on the lookout for bears and take precautions so as to neither attract nor antagonize those which might be in the area. The following are good practices to carry out when in bear country:

— When hiking, stay in a group.
— Leave your dog at home.
— Keep in the open, where possible.
— Avoid favorite bear food sources such as berry patches and carcasses.
— When travelling through forested stretches, try carrying a noisemaker such as bells.
— Always be on the lookout for bear sign such as tracks, droppings and diggings.
— When canoeing in shallow water, remember that a bear can move faster through the water than a canoeist.
— If you catch sight of a bear, never feed or harass him or go near a cub.
— Go out of your way to avoid a black bear; leave the area at once if there is a grizzly in the vicinity.
— Food should never be cooked or stored in a tent, but is best either locked in a vehicle or stored in a pack suspended from a tree. If there are no tall trees around cache the food well away from camp.
— Dirty utensils or garbage should not be left around a campsite.
— Garbage should be burned and all non-combustible material packed out.
— In the case of an attack by a bear, your best chance is to keep calm and assess your situation. Never run. Experts advise that you try speaking softly, back slowly toward a tree, and then climb it. If there are no trees and you are being charged, a last resort might be to play dead, with legs bent up to protect the chest and hands clasped behind the neck.

OUTDOOR ETHICS

The outdoorsperson has a moral responsibility, not only to himself or herself but also to other people and to the environment. The following are a few points which relate to a canoeing experience:

— Divide large groups of canoeists into small parties for travelling and camping together, as this will make it easier for members of the group to keep track of one another, and will minimize congestion and environmental damage.
— Ask permission to land, cross, or camp on private property.
— Camp in one place for only a short time.
— For firewood use only the lower dead branches from large trees - do not damage live trees.
— On well travelled routes such as the Yukon, only build a fire when necessary, and then only with wood that can easily be collected by hand. A small gas stove is faster, easier, and less damaging to the environment.
— Be aware of fire restrictions and be certain that fires are put out. Fire permits are required for fires anywhere other than in a government campground; free permits can be obtained from the R.C.M.P., Forest Service or Game Branch.
— Do not disturb or remove artifacts or items of historical interest.
— Observe fishing and hunting regulations.
— Carry out all garbage that cannot be burned.

Mountain Goat with Kids.

ROUTES

Following are the canoe routes of the Yukon Territory. There is a route index on page 3 and an alphabetical index on page 110.

All measurements have been given in the metric system. However since many people will still be using miles rather than kilometres, especially in driving distances, here are some formulas for changing from metric to the Old English system:

Kilometres to miles $= km \times 0.621$
Metres to feet $= m \times 3.281$
Centimetres to inches $= cm \times 0.4$
Hectares to acres $= hectares \times 2.471$
Celsius to Fahrenheit $= c \times 1.8 + 32$

n/a indicates information not available at time of printing. N.T.S. is an abbreviation for National Topographic Series.

Note: Maps are intended for area reference only. The suggested topographic sheets should be purchased for the actual journey.

Topographical maps of any area of the Yukon may be purchased from:
Geological Survey of Canada
P.O. Box 969
Whitehorse, Y.T.

Topographical maps of the Yukon and British Columbia may be purchased from:
Geological Survey of Canada
Information Services
6th Floor, 100 West Pender
Vancouver, B.C.

Topographical maps of Alaska may be purchased from:
U.S Geological Survey
Map Sales Office
508 West Second Avenue
Anchorage, Alaska 99501

River routes in the Yukon vary from those suitable for novice paddlers through to those suitable for expert paddlers in closed boats, with extensive wilderness experience. Those generally recognized as suitable for novices, include the Yukon, Stewart, Teslin, Nisutlin and some of the smaller lakes. Only expert paddlers competent in route research, preparation and ability to meet all wilderness eventualities should even consider routes like the Peel, Alsek and Blow.

The route descriptions that follow should in all cases be taken only as a general guide to river conditions. A year of high water or scouring from ice break-up may create new rapids, eliminate sandbars, change formerly safe passages such as chutes, and completely alter certain sections of the river. In addition you may be travelling the river at a water level different from the route description.

A Bush Plane.

Lower water levels are usually safer but more difficult to navigate. The current is slower with fewer boils, surges and eddies. Higher water will be faster with an increase in boils, surges and eddies, more powerful haystacks, and more souse holes. As high water usually occurs immediately following spring break-up, the river will have a higher silt content and more floating debris such as driftwood, uprooted trees and sweepers. The more powerful, faster current may make it difficult to avoid these obstacles. On the plus side, high water tends to drown out rock gardens and some rapids, and provides more water in which to maneuver.

Distance travelled per day on a river will obviously depend on the interests and capabilities of paddlers as well as on the peculiarities of the river. On large rivers with a current of 8 km/h or faster, 80 to 95 kilometres per day is a good average. On slow rivers, with large meander bends and slack water, 30 to 50 kilometres per day might be average. Lake paddling will be considerably slower. At the beginning of a trip, when muscles are still tightening, a 22 km lake paddle will be doing well. Paddling can be physically demanding and use up a large amount of energy, as with any type of physical labour, and an eight hour day will be a good days work.

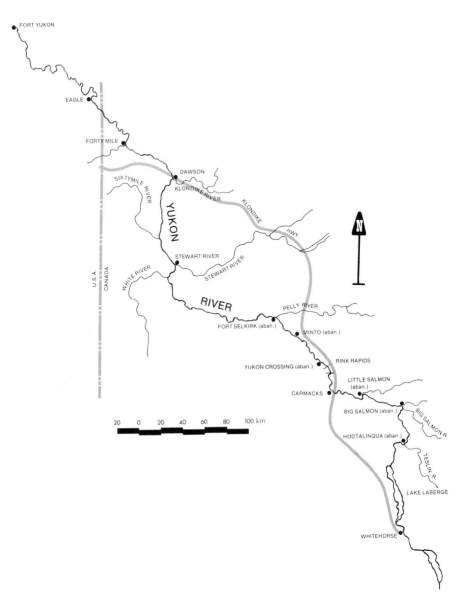

ROUTE - YUKON RIVER - MARSH LAKE, Y.T. TO EAGLE, ALASKA
GRADE - *1 to 2*
LENGTH - *900 km*
WIDTH - *15 m to 500 m*
VERTICAL DROP - *Approx. 335 m*
TIME TO ALLOW - *2 to 3 weeks*
NEAREST EMERGENCY COMMUNICATION -
Whitehorse, Carmacks, Minto, Fort Selkirk, Dawson City, Eagle Alaska

CAMPING - ACCOMMODATION - *Accommodation at Whitehorse, Carmacks, Dawson City and Eagle; Camping unorganized but easy along route*

MAPS - *N.T.S. 1:250,000 105D Whitehorse; 105E Laberge; 105L Glenlyon; 115I Carmacks: 115J Snag; 115O Stewart River; 116B,C Dawson*

HAZARDS - *Few. Wilderness, but well travelled*

DIRECTIONS

Put-in at Tagish, McClintock or Whitehorse, Yukon Territory, and take-out at Dawson, Y.T., or Eagle, Alaska, just west of the Canadian - U.S.A. border.

DESCRIPTION

There are two ways, at least, of describing river trips. The first is to tell the reader everything possible about the route, a complete bend by bend account, listing all tributaries, points of interest, cabins, wrecks, rapids, riffles and rough spots. The second, and the way we have chosen, is to give the reader enough information to make the trip comfortable, safe and interesting. Discovery should be a part of any wilderness trip, as research should. Knowing the location of too many places detracts from this experience. This description and good topo sheets will allow you to embark on a journey of discovery. If you want more information look up the history books in the bibliography. If you want a bend by bend description we can recommend three other reading sources.

The first, and most useful is a river chart, similar to that used by the stern-wheelers. Originally this was a lineal chart on two rollers. Now it is a lineal chart, but read page by page. An updated chart has been published by Bruce Batchelor of Whitehorse and is available from the Whitehorse Star. These maps show the river in great detail and include a great deal of information, such as the location of wrecks, wood cutters camps and old trading posts.

Two guide books to the river have been published. The one, available from Alaska magazine, entitled *A Boater's Guide to the Upper Yukon River,* is a slim volume with some good notes about what is to be found along the route. The other, *The Yukon River Trail Guide,* by Archie Satterfield, is more complete but has two major annoyances. The first is that it was written for people from the U.S.A. specifically and therefore has an information bias. The second is that the author is not a canoeist and motored down the river. It misses the intimate association that it might have had if written by a paddler.

The Yukon River is one of the longest in North America, over 3200 km in length from its birthplace in the British Columbia mountains to its mouth in the Bering Sea of Alaska. It's lure to canoeists though is not just its length but the fact that here is a lineal museum of history, geology and natural history, an easy route to discovering something of one's country, and oneself.

It has been said that this great river was probably the first to be discovered by North American man, as he originally migrated across the Bering Straits, and the last great river to be "discovered" or explored by European or non-native man in the time of written history. It was not until 1835 that a Russian trader travelling overland from Norton Sound stumbled on a large river that he called the Kwikpak. Robert Campbell of the H.B.C. found the Pelly and then in 1843 travelled down it to its confluence with another large river, that he named the Lewes. In 1845 John Bell, following orders to explore the Porcupine, travelled downstream to a large river, which he called the Youcon, a name given it by the local Indians. A post was built here in 1847 and one at Fort Selkirk on the Lewes in 1848. It took three more years to discover that these two posts were on the same river, and that this was the river the Russian traders in Alaska called the Kwikpak. Later, of course, it all became the Yukon; except that some people still call the lower section the Kwikpak, and some maps still name the upper part the Lewes; or the Thirty Mile, or Fifty Mile.

For fifty years little happened on this river of the north. Trading posts, missions and a few prospectors, adventurers, geographers and explorers wandered up and down but generally things were pretty quiet. Then in 1897 a prospector named Bob Henderson found some gold showing on Bonanza creek. It was not a rich strike but looked promising. He passed this information to George Carmack who was camped with his friends Skookum Jim and Tagish Charlie. Weeks later, almost by accident, the three found a rich strike. Forgetting, or not bothering to tell Henderson of this new find, they staked their claims and the rush for the Klondike was on. By the time Henderson heard of the strike all the claims were staked.

The Klondike rush opened up the Yukon country, but the river has almost reverted to its natural state. For years it was the main means of transportation. During the Second World War it was superceded by roads, and to a great extent by air travel. So the sternwheelers were beached, the wood cutters moved on to other places and the river became quiet again. In recent years it has begun to be a popular recreation route for boaters, and one particularly suited to paddles as a means of locomotion.

Canoeists should remember that this is a wilderness river, and although there are large numbers of people travelling the water they are spread over 800 km. Travel as you would in any wilderness area, with a certain amount of caution and fully prepared.

The Yukon is usually described in sections, based on the various access points. We will do the same, breaking it into easily travelled segments.

There are several places to start a Yukon trip, one being the Chilkoot trail and another Carcross, but both of these entail travelling on large open bodies of water that are unsuitable to canoes. Whitehorse misses the upper river, so Marsh Lake is a good compromise. The first thing to do at Tagish Crossing is visit Tagish Anne's bakery. Travelling up the Alaska Highway allows few places to find anything fresh so Anne's is a welcome change. Put-in on Marsh Lake at Tagish Narrows, where the long wooden bridge crosses the lake at the Yukon Government campground. This lake was called Mud Lake by the early trappers and miners, an apt name that was changed when Lieut. Schwatka of the U.S. Army passed this way naming everything in sight. Marsh came from Professor O.C. Marsh, an American scientist. The lake is approximately 32 km long.

At the northern end Marsh Lake is drained by the upper Yukon, called the Lewes on many maps. There are no obstacles until 11 km, where a dam crosses. There is a set of locks on the right side which allows passage. Paddle to the left when leaving the lock to avoid back eddies. The river changes now, being swifter and narrower as it flows toward Miles Canyon.

About 18 km from the dam was the site of Canyon City where Klondikers stopped to portage equipment or prepared to run Miles Canyon. Little remains of the city, and Miles Canyon has been tamed by a downstream dam. The canyon can now be run, but there are some eddies and whirlpools from the steep walls and fast water. Scout it to decide if you really want to run through. Below the Canyon is Schwatka Lake, formed by a power dam at Whitehorse rapids. The dam will have to be portaged, usually accomplished with the aid of a cab or friendly trucker.

Below Whitehorse, the capital of the Yukon Territory, the Lewes changes. Now it is about 200 metres wide with scattered islands and gravel banks. White spruce and poplar are along the shore, and lodgepole pine on the hills above. Don't drink the water. Whitehorse's sewage has been added to the flow. This is a pleasant trip, and a scenic one, that leads to Lake Laberge.

A note about the cabins and historic sites you may visit: all of these are protected by the Yukon Territorial Government. It is unlawful to destroy or remove anything. Empty and open cabins may be used for shelter.

There are a few navigational hazards on the right as Lake Laberge is entered. Wing dams were built here to try and force the river into one channel, thereby making it easier for sternwheelers to navigate the shallows. Watch for winds on the lake and stay close to shore. It is 51 km long.

The section of river below Lake Laberge is often referred to as the Thirty Mile, meaning the thirty mile stretch from the lake to the mouth of the Teslin. For this distance the river is about 20 metres wide with a speed of 5 to 7 km/h, and no rapids. Several old wood camps are seen in this section and at least one steamer was sunk, near the mouth of Domville Creek. Wildlife and birdlife is particularly abundant along here. Moose, bear and wolves may be seen, and water fowl such as canvasbacks, mallards, wood ducks, and geese. Eagles often soar overhead. Campsites are easily found.

At the mouth of the Teslin River is the site of Hootalinqua, an Indian village and former roadhouse for a shipyard that was built here. 1.5 km downstream the steamer *Evylyn* is in drydock, and a little further at Scow Bay, the old steamer *Klondike* has drifted onto a gravel bar.

With the inflow of the Teslin the river is now wider and deeper, and once again drinkable. River banks are lower and the water a browner color. Big Salmon River is the next stopping point. It was at one time an R.C.M.P. post, on the left side, and on the right an Indian village. From here to Little Salmon there are several cabins along the shore and an old gold dredge on

Five Finger Rapids on The Yukon.

the river bank. Little Salmon is reached 260 km from Whitehorse. It is on the right bank of the river just downstream of the mouth of the Little Salmon River.

Leaving the abandoned Indian village of Little Salmon canoeists will probably notice the sound of traffic. From here to Carmacks the highway is nearby. Lakeview, a few km downstream, on the left has a few good cabins left. Then the river makes some large meander bends, passes through an area known as Columbia Slough and heads for Carmacks. This small town is the half way point to Dawson City, and is heralded by a bridge crossing the river carrying the Whitehorse to Dawson Highway. Most services are available here. In fact this is your last chance before Dawson City to purchase supplies. It would be a good idea to check in with the R.C.M.P. here before continuing. Access to the town is easy from a number of roads. Dawson City is 415 km downstream.

The river below Carmacks has the first set of rapids on the Yukon River, Five Finger Rapids. They are easily run on the right, through a few small waves and some exciting fast water. Aligning should take place near the old winch house which once pulled streamers up through the swift sections.

Just downstream are Rink Rapids, the last on the river. Rocks that at one time hindered steamers were blasted out of the way. There are whitewater sections here but they may be avoided, unless you prefer a more exciting ride. At least two sternwheelers were sunk here.

Yukon Crossing is an old crossing point of the stage line from Whitehorse to Dawson City. Some old buildings remain. A slough nearby makes a good swimming hole.

Further downstream is Minto, but unfortunately the old buildings of the church and trading post have been destroyed by transients. The highway, an emergency landing strip and a Yukon Government Campground are within a kilometre of the river.

At the mouth of the Pelly River, Robert Campbell established Fort Selkirk in 1848. When he found this site subject to flooding he moved across the river to the left bank. In 1852 the fort was attacked by hostile Indians and much of it destroyed. The post was abandoned and later burnt. Years later it was re-established with a mission, R.C.M.P. post and a trading post. There is now a caretaker there to look after the buildings. This is a good place to stop and explore for awhile.

The 150 km from here to White River is one of the most interesting for anyone interested in historic artifacts. There are many wood camps and old mines along the river, as well as trail heads to various placer mines and gold rushes, and trading posts that at one time served river travellers. Travel slowly and explore in detail. The scenery is excellent and the paddling easy.

At White River, named for the color of the water which is filled with glacial silt and volcanic ash, the river widens to about 2 km. Floating debris becomes more common and there are many islands and bars in the river. Points of interest in the 128 km from the White to Dawson include a small General Store at the mouth of the Stewart River, once the site of a town; the site of the first post office in the Yukon at Ogilvie Island, directly opposite the mouth of the Sixtymile River, and several old cabins and camps. Good camping is located at a point 0.5 km up the Sixtymile River.

The Sixtymile is named for its distance from Fort Reliance, which is just a few km below Dawson. It makes a good point to camp before what is the final run to Dawson for most paddlers.

Dawson is the take-out point for most paddlers, but even if you plan on continuing down the river you should spend a day or two here. It was built at the beginning of the Klondike gold rush of 1897-98 and is in the process of being restored. There are many places to explore, and visit, and some interesting side trips around the area. All services and supplies are available here.

Dawson is the easiest point to take-out. If you decide to continue on the river to the border then you should check with customs. The next take-out is at Eagle, Alaska, about 160 km downstream. There is road access to that point. Of course it is possible to continue even further, to Circle, Alaska, or Fort Yukon or even the Bering Sea. However egress is much more difficult from these places.

The river is easy paddling below Dawson though the current begins to slow somewhat. There are some shallows and lots of islands and sandbars. Both the valley and the river widen as the border is approached and mountains become more evident in the distance.

Fortymile is one of the major places still left to visit on this section of river. A description of this area is given under the Fortymile River route. Other settlements have been long abandoned and little remains. The border is marked by a wide slash through the bush and a small monument on the river bank. The end of the journey at Eagle is just downstream round a bend in the river. An Indian village is on the left upstream of the town. Eagle is on the left bank also. There is good road access here. Remember to check with customs and the R.C.M.P. at the end of your trip.

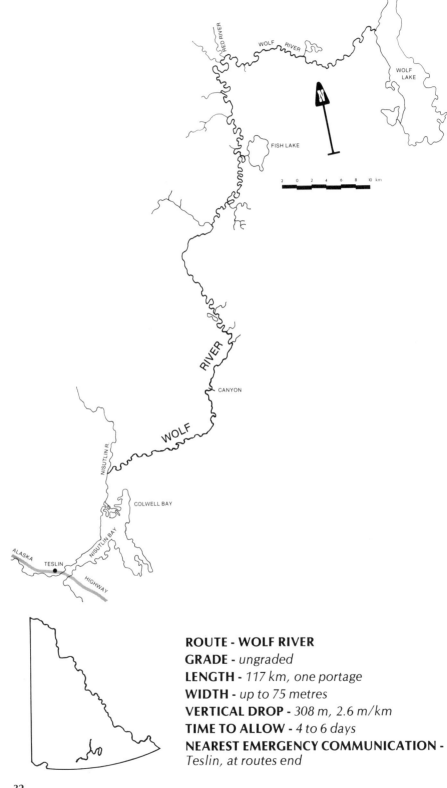

ROUTE - WOLF RIVER
GRADE - *ungraded*
LENGTH - *117 km, one portage*
WIDTH - *up to 75 metres*
VERTICAL DROP - *308 m, 2.6 m/km*
TIME TO ALLOW - *4 to 6 days*
NEAREST EMERGENCY COMMUNICATION -
Teslin, at routes end

CAMPING - ACCOMMODATION - *Unorganized*
MAPS - *N.T.S 1:250,000 105B Wolf Lake; 105C Teslin*
HAZARDS - *Route uncharted, remote*

DIRECTIONS

Access is by flying in to Wolf Lake at river's head, or to Fish Lake, 45 km downstream. Take-out is at Teslin.

DESCRIPTION

Available information on the Wolf River, which lies to the east of Teslin Lake and drains into the Nisutlin, is scanty, so any canoe trip would be somewhat exploratory in nature. It is reported to be canoeable for its complete length with just one portage past a canyon that lies 24 km from its mouth, or 35 from Fish Lake. Near its mouth the river is about a metre deep with a speed of 13 km/h.

Access to the river is from Wolf Lake which lies at an elevation of 990 metres 85 km west and north of Watson Lake. An alternate launching site would be from Fish Lake, 45 km downstream. There is a 1 km stream that empties Fish Lake into the Wolf River.

For the first part of its journey the river flows in a large bend around the north end of the Englishman's Range of mountains. Then it turns west to flow into the Nisutlin, 15 km from Teslin. At its headwaters the lake is only 3 metres lower than Morris Lake, and just a few kilometres north of the headwaters of the Moberly River. In a heavy rain the swamp that divides the two drainages must almost flow each way. The Moberly too flows into Teslin Lake by taking a southerly course around the Englishman's Range.

Vegetation and wildlife will be similar to that found in the Nisutlin drainage.

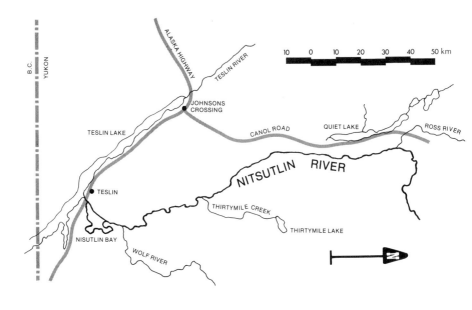

ROUTE - NISUTLIN RIVER
GRADE - *1+*
LENGTH - *180 km*
WIDTH - *30 to 100 m*
VERTICAL DROP - *100 m; 3 decimetres/km*
TIME TO ALLOW - *4 days to 1 week*
NEAREST EMERGENCY COMMUNICATION -
Teslin, Johnson's Crossing,
Quiet Lake Campground
CAMPING - ACCOMMODATION - *Quiet Lake Campground, Mile 47*
Canol Road. Unorganized along route, but many excellent sites.
MAPS - *N.T.S 1:250,000 105F Quiet Lake; 105C Teslin*
HAZARDS - *Remote area*

DIRECTIONS

Automobile access from Mile 42 of the Canol Road. Take-out at Teslin.

DIRECTIONS

If the prospective canoeist turns his vehicle northeast from the Alaska Highway at Johnson's Crossing, Mile 836, onto the Canol Road, he will discover that he has a choice of two excellent canoe trips to choose between. One, described elsewhere in this book, leads from Quiet Lake at Mile 46 of the Canol Road down the Big Salmon River to the Yukon River. The other route goes the opposite direction from Mile 42, ending 180 km away at Nisutlin Bay on Teslin Lake, about 15 km from the town of Teslin. This route is of course the Nisutlin River.

Unlike many routes in the Yukon this one does not require an expensive flight into the back country, nor does it require that the canoeist be an expert paddler. Certainly canoeists should have some river experience and be familiar with wilderness though. It is considered an easy trip suitable for most competent paddlers.

The Canol Road, which gives access to the river's headwaters, was built as a military project during WWII. Its purpose was to connect oil fields at Norman Wells on the Mackenzie River, in the Northwest Territories, with a refinery at Whitehorse. The refinery was abandoned and torn down after only 2 years of service, and some years ago the pipe was torn up. The road remains as a scenic recreational road for summer travellers.

At Mile 47 of the road, on Quiet Lake, the Yukon Government has a camp-ground. This makes a good base camp for the trip. Motorists should arrange to leave their vehicle with someone in Johnson's Crossing or Teslin and arrange for a ride to the starting point at Mile 42. An alternate starting point would be to travel down the Ross River to the Nisutlin. The Ross is crossed by the Canol Road just after it swings away from Quiet Lake.

One of the first mentions of the Nisutlin River is in George Dawson's report of his exploration of the Yukon in 1887. At the mouth of the Teslin River he met a miner named Boswell who told him that the main tributary of Teslin Lake was a river known to the Tagish Indians as Ni-sutlin-Hi-Ni. He said it rose between the Big Salmon and Pelly Rivers and flowed in a southerly direction into the lake. Along it he said the Indians had two fishing stations for salmon.

The river did not however prove to be a gold-bearing stream and so like the Big Salmon it was left relatively untouched by the gold rush. Today it is still used by Indians, who come up from the town of Teslin to hunt and trap in the valley. Their cabins will occasionally be seen along the river. Other signs of humanity along the route include some areas cleared by log-ging near Nisutlin Bay, and an abandoned sawmill on the east shore of the river about 20 km below Thirty Mile Creek.

At the put-in there is a good camping area, flat and dry with lots of fire-wood. At this point the river is about 35 metres wide, and 2.5 to 3 metres deep in the middle, with a velocity of 6 or 7 km/h. The first 30 km of the trip offer the canoeist a wide variety of scenery, vegetation and wildlife. Willow, alder and aspen line the banks with white spruce in the valley and lodgepole pine on the hills Glide quietly in the morning and evening hours and watch for moose, Canada geese, beaver and ducks. During salmon runs in the late summer watch for, and pay caution to, black and grizzly bears. Bald eagles also nest along the river. It is an excellent fishing river, particularly for grayling.

Below the launching point the river gradually deepens, becoming more cloudy from slides in the sand and gravel cutbanks. Drinking water though is easily obtained from the numerous side streams entering the Nisutlin. These are also often good for short side trips.

The cutbanks average 30 m in height, and are usually topped with tall lodgepole pine. One of these, called "Roaring Bull" by the locals, is worth noting. It is located about 16 km below the put-in point, and features a U-shaped bend and a high bank. When the river is high, water surges around the bend creating boils; at low water it is merely swift.

The valley increases from 3 km in width to 6 or 7 km when one is 25 km below the access point. The sand and gravel cutbanks end, and the banks become lower. Sweepers will be encountered along the shores here, but since the river is 60 m wide there is no danger. The current becomes slower here, and the river begins to meander more.

About 20 km above the mouth of Thirty Mile Creek the river valley becomes narrower, and remains this way until 8 km above the creek. On the hills on each side of the river the layering of the different types of vegetation are very noticeable. The banks are lined with alder, willow, and aspen; white spruce covers the slopes above; the ridges above are topped with lodgepole pine.

When the river valley widens again just before Thirty Mile Creek the surrounding land becomes quite marshy. A curious characteristic of this area is that the shore, which rises about 2 m above the water, extends back from the river only 100 m or so before it drops off into marshland. This is most marked on the east side of the river. The banks become very muddy, and landing here is often difficult. When the shore slopes gently to the river, however, the tops of these banks make good potential campsites.

Thirty Mile Creek, entering from the left, causes no turbulence or other difficulties. Below it the Nisutlin Valley narrows once again to 4 km; it widens again to 8 km just before it reaches Nisutlin Bay. The river is about 90 m wide here, and is quite swampy. The current slows to about 1 to 2 km per hour.

Open areas will be seen through the trees above the banks; there are many small lakes which drain into the Nisutlin hidden behind the shore. One worth noting - and the 100 m walk - is to be found 13.5 km above Wolf River on the east bank. Campsites are best located among the frequent stands of poplar lining the banks. Campers here will be able to gaze at the snow-capped peaks of the Big Salmon Range 10 km away, and also at the 2000 m Dawson Peaks, 50 km away in British Columbia.

The marshy areas end about 1.5 km above Wolf River. The east shore becomes a steep 10 m sand and gravel slope topped with pine and spruce, while the gradually rising banks on the west are completely covered with spruce. The wet areas inshore from the river disappear.

Just below the mouth of the clear and swift Wolf River the canoeist will encounter the only real rapids in the Nisutlin. They are about 2.5 km long and present no danger. Rather, they make a pleasant change from the slow meanders of the last kilometers. The river narrows to 35 or 40 m, and the current increases to 10 km per hour.

These rapids are comprised of two sections, with quieter water in between. The first should be run straight down the middle. A short way below this section are two islands; on the far right of these are rapids which are mainly swells as the river flows over large rocks. This rapid can be avoided by taking the left channel past the islands; the rapid, however, really poses no threat even to novice canoeists. When going through the rapids, stay on the extreme right to avoid the shallow water near the islands.

Cleared areas, debris, and log piles near the waters edge are indications of civilization as one nears Nisutlin Bay. The river branches into a delta as it enters the bay, with the forks separated by grass and brush covered islands. This is a nesting ground for Canada geese.

Once through the delta, it is a paddle of about 15 km to the town of Teslin. The right shore of the bay is heavily overgrown, and strewn with logs and driftwood. It is important to plan this stretch, as there do not appear to be any good camping places along the shore.

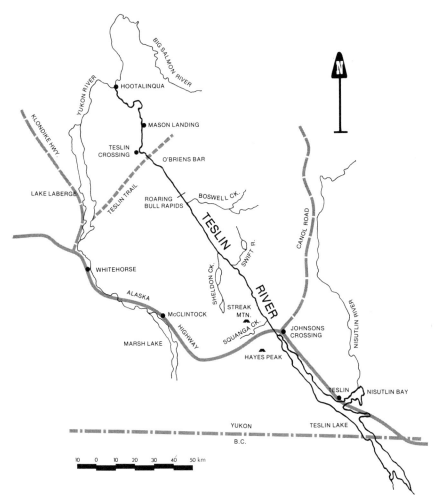

ROUTE - TESLIN RIVER

GRADE - *Lake, river 1 to 2, rapids to 3*

LENGTH - *Teslin to Yukon River 230 km
Teslin to Carmacks 420 km*

WIDTH - *Teslin Lake 500 m to 3.5 km;
River 50 to 500 m; average 150 m*

VERTICAL DROP - *60 m to Yukon River;
Teslin Lake elevation 683 m*

TIME TO ALLOW - *2 weeks*

NEAREST EMERGENCY COMMUNICATION -
Teslin, Johnson's Crossing, Carmacks

CAMPING - ACCOMMODATION - *Campsites and services at Teslin,
Johnson's Crossing and Carmacks. Remainder of route unorganized*

MAPS - *N.T.S. 1:250,000 105C Teslin: 105D Whitehorse; 105E Laberge;
105L Glenlyon; 115I Carmacks*

HAZARDS - *Remote*

DIRECTIONS

Access at Teslin, Mile 804 of Alaska Highway, or at Johnson's Crossing, Mile 837. Access also possible at Morley Bay, Mile 794 but no services. Head of Teslin Lake accessible only by air or boat. Take-out at Carmacks, Mile 102 of Klondike Highway on Yukon River.

DESCRIPTION

Compared to many of the canoe routes possible in the Yukon, the Teslin Lake and River trip is relatively easy. There are no difficult rapids, and no portages to make. The route is made even more attractive by its ease of access, and by the excellent fishing available.

While it is possible to fly in to the head of Teslin Lake, south in British Columbia, most canoeists begin at the town of Teslin. Those wishing to bypass 50 km of lake and travel only the river can put-in at Johnson's Crossing.

Teslin, originally Tes-lin-too, is reported to mean "long waters" in the dialect of the Indians who lived at the village of Nisutlin on the east shore of the lake. The lake was known to exist by the 1850's and was at that time thought to be the headwaters of the Yukon River. When gold was discovered on Klondike Creek in 1896 Teslin Lake and River became one of the routes used to reach the goldfields. From Wrangell, Alaska, in the panhandle, sternwheelers brought miners up the Stikine River to Telegraph Creek. From there the men walked the old telegraph trail to the head of the lake and built rafts or boats to float them downstream to the Yukon River. At Nisutlin, a village of the Inland Tlingit Indians a settlement grew, serving as a supply point for the miners. Other stopping points included Johnson's Crossing, McClintock, Teslin Crossing, Mason Landing and Hootalinqua. Only Teslin and Johnson's Crossing have survived, due to their locations on the Alaska Highway.

The scenery for canoeists as they begin this trip is both beautiful and spectacular. The west shore of the lake rises from park-like sand and gravel beaches through clear flat areas of spruce and poplar to rolling hills forested with white spruce and lodgepole pine. This side of the lake offers many beautiful campsites. By comparision the eastern shore appears barren; it is higher, with many rocky outcroppings and bald peaks. Along the lake thick willow growth to the highwater mark eliminates the beaches found on the western shore. The Dawson Peaks (elevation 1920 m) loom to the south at the Yukon - British Columbia Boundary. The impressive dome rising 1850 m toward the end of the lake to the west is Hayes Peak, also known as old Baldy. It is named after Charles Willard Hayes, a field geologist with the American Schwatka Expedition that travelled the length of the Yukon in 1891. In two portable canoes they travelled down Teslin Lake and River in 12 days.

The ardent fisherman might never leave Teslin Lake to explore the river below. Oblivious to the scenery, he will be getting his limit of grayling and lake trout off the sandy west shore beaches. Fishing starts in Teslin Lake when the ice goes out in early June and is good through to September. Trolling is the most effective means. Lake trout from 2 to 8 kilograms can

Teslin River.

be caught with large lures like a red and white, silver and bronze or a "Half Wave". Grayling to 1 kilogram are best caught with a black gnat fly or spinners. As well there are inconnu, northern pike and whitefish and salmon.

Most travellers in canoes will leave the lake to continue following the ghosts of the men lured by mystical gold, on toward the Yukon. Gradually the lake narrows as it becomes the Teslin River. About 5 km before Johnson's Crossing it is approximately 500 metres wide and a gentle current becomes noticeable. Here, between the eroding clay river banks, the river is crossed by the immense Johnson's Crossing bridge. This bridge was built with an extremely high clearance in order to allow steamers of the British Yukon Navigation Company to pass on their route from Teslin to Whitehorse. These steamers were retired in 1942 when the highway provided a faster and more economical means of freighting. Watch for swallows nests under the bridge.

A Yukon government campsite is located on the west bank of the river below the bridge. This is the put-in point for those who only want to travel the river. There is a restaurant, gas station and lodging at Johnson's Crossing.

About 5 km downstream of the bridge the river makes a sharp bend to the right, and the current increases to 4-6 km per hour. There are some easy rapids here that require no special maneuvering. The river then makes a turn to the left, and opens up into a wide area of sloughs, with high wood banks behind both shores. This is a good area to observe waterfowl and other small songbirds; moose may also be seen, particularly in the early and late part of the day. For anglers the Teslin River is one of the best in the north for grayling.

Squanga Creek, entering from the left about 10 km below Johnson's Crossing, marks the end of the sloughs and the beginning of the narrowing of the river. Squanga Creek is navigable upstream for almost a kilometre before very swift rapids are encountered. Wild rice is abundant at the confluence of the creek and river.

The physical characteristics of the river change drastically 10 km below Squanga Creek. The Teslin widens to over 300 metres and the clear water slows to 1-3 km per hour. The east bank now forms a terrace; forested in spruce it cuts the traveller off from the clay banks of the last few kilometres. The rounded foothills of the Big Salmon Range can be seen in the distance. The west shore consists of three to four levels which rise gradually to high wooded hillsides. The river gradually narrows over the next 10 km, and the current increases again. There are a variety of digressions possible on this part of the route with several accessible lagoons on both sides of the river. These are good areas to observe and photograph wildlife such as moose and bear. Watch for beavers.

Several kilometres before Swift River enters the Teslin from the right, the river narrows to 60 to 90 metres, and the current increases noticeably to 6 or 7 km/h. Clay hoodoo-like features line the east bank. There is good camping sites at the mouth of the Swift River and though the water is fast swimmers will appreciate its warmer water.

For the next 24 km the river meanders through high clay banks backed by high wooded hills. The water, flowing at about 6 km/h becomes quite murky here, as the clay banks are unstable and large slides are common. Below this section the river narrows to 100 to 125 metres and the surrounding land becomes lower. Sandy beaches become more common, and there are small islands in the river.

Below Sheldon Creek, which enters from the left, the water velocity increases to approximately 10 km/h. Stay to the right of mid-stream to avoid riffles and surges near Boswell Creek. The creek, and a mountain that can be seen downstream, Mount Boswell, are named for Thomas Boswell, a miner who was prospecting this area before 1887.

The only large rapids on the Teslin occur several kilometres below Sheldon Creek. Their onset is marked by a horseshoe bend to the right with a very high and steep cut-bank. These rapids, known as Roaring Bull Rapids, are very swift with water that appears to roll over riverbed obstructions, creating swells and some breaking waves. They are, however, free of obstructions, and are straight forward canoeing. Those who wish to avoid much of the fast water should go to the right of the island located just before the high banks of the rapids.

The river remains narrow from below the rapids until about 8 km below the site of Teslin Crossing, the place where the old Teslin Trail forded the river. Hikers will enjoy going ashore here to explore some of the old trails.

A spectacular clay bank, 100 to 130 metres high, located a few kilometres below the trail crossing is a good area to watch for bald eagles. At this point the purplish Semenof Hills come into view, their name a reminder of the first traders who established in Alaska. This is another good area for hiking. On the other side of the Semenof Hills is the Big Salmon River.

Ten km before Mason Landing there is evidence of a fairly recent burn and on the west shore considerable evidence of beaver activity. Mason Landing, on the right bank, is the site of an old steamer landing.

While the river widens around several islands, it averages 150 metres in width as it gently rolls into the section of Yukon River known as the Thirty Mile. At this point the silty water becomes a beautiful turquoise. A good view of the west bank of the Yukon River and the abandoned site of Hootalinqua can be had from the alder and willow covered spit which separates the two rivers. The site is an interesting place to explore and is described further under the Yukon trip.

At this point the canoeist has covered approximately half of the trip to Carmacks. The latter half is found in the section of this book on the Yukon River.

The Steamer Tarahne *beached at Atlin.*

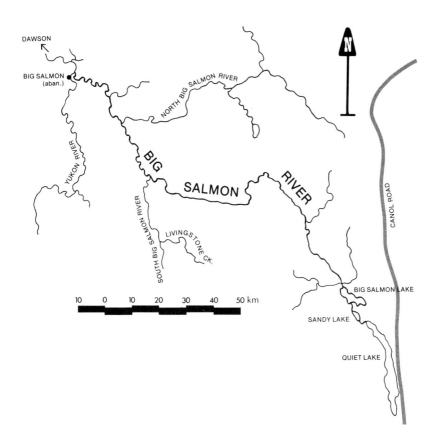

ROUTE - BIG SALMON RIVER
GRADE - *1 to 2, rapids to 4*
LENGTH - *Quiet Lake to Yukon River - 275 km*
Quiet Lake to Carmacks - 400 km
WIDTH - *25 m to 4 km at Quiet Lake*
VERTICAL DROP - *300 m*
TIME TO ALLOW - *10 days to Carmacks*
NEAREST EMERGENCY COMMUNICATION -
Johnson's Crossing, Quiet Lake and Carmacks
CAMPING - ACCOMMODATION - *Yukon Government campground at Quiet Lake; unorganized along route*
MAPS - *N.T.S. 1:250,000 105F Quiet Lake; 105E Laberge*
HAZARDS - *Remote, long rapids, sweepers, occasional log jams*

DIRECTIONS

Put-in at Quiet Lake, Mile 47 on Canol Road. Take-out at Carmacks on Yukon River.

DESCRIPTION

The Big Salmon is one of those unique rivers that offers something for almost every canoeist. The fisherman will find grayling in abundance in almost all parts of the river system; the recreational camper will find unspoiled wilderness; the photographer will find beautiful scenery and plentiful wildlife; the novice can paddle on lakes and placid river; the expert can attack some moderate rapids.

Rapids? Don't panic! While some of the rapids on the Big Salmon are quite long, and do make up a large percentage of the trip, they do not present any difficulty if approached with care. There is always ample warning when one nears them and they may be scouted as one canoes nearer. There is no difficulty aligning for the runs. Widely spaced boulders are easily avoided, as are gravel bars. These may be more of a hazard when the water level is low.

Like the Nisutlin River the Big Salmon was untouched by the rush for Yukon gold and therefore has remained in a relatively primitive state. One of its tributaries did have gold though, the South Big Salmon which joins the Big Salmon a little over half way to the Yukon. Near the headwaters of this river was Livingstone Creek, which between 1897 and 1900 produced more than $2 million in gold. There was an R.C.M.P. post, a trading post and the miners cabins. It was reached by a trail from Lake Laberge, across the Teslin River and the Semenof Hills to the South Big Salmon River. There is still some mining there today. The mainstream though has remained quiet.

The Big Salmon trip begins at Quiet Lake. This is easily reached by taking the Canol Road from Johnson's Crossing, Mile 836 on the Alaska Highway. An alternative would be to fly into Quiet Lake by floatplane, although one of the appeals of the Big Salmon is the easy access. Quiet Lake is 31 km long and 4 km wide at its widest point. The high mountains of the Big Salmon Range border the lake to the west, while to the east is the rolling plain that stretches to the Nisutlin River.

After paddling to the north end of Quiet Lake, the canoeist enters a stream leading to Sandy Lake. This shallow, narrow waterway is about 2 km long, with a current ranging from 3 to 10 km per hour. It is difficult to get ashore as the banks are lined with a tangle of willows.

Sandy Lake, surrounded by high wooded hills, is about 3.5 km long. A stream running from the north end joins it to Big Salmon Lake, 5 km away. The lakes and rivers by the way, are named for the size of the fish. The stream enters Big Salmon Lake in the middle of the southern shore, 6 km from the start of the Big Salmon River.

Big Salmon Lake, like the river, is surrounded by mountains. The river valley, at times as narrow at 500 metres, flows through a range of mountains that are 1200 to 1500 metres high, with some peaks over 1800 metres. Strangely enough these are called the Big Salmon Range. The steep terraces between the banks and the mountains are the habitat of moose and black bear, often seen by the canoeist. Along the river canoeists may also see Canada geese, ducks beaver and bald eagles. Because of the small number of humans using the river system wildlife tends to be very curious. Remember that these "tame" moose and bear can be dangerous.

The banks of the Big Salmon River do not offer many places to camp. Gravel bars and beaches are good potential sites, as are islands. Camping in the open will minimize insect bites.

The river banks are generally sloughing and therefore sweepers are common. The swiftest sections of the river occur on the outside of bends, with back eddies located on the downstream side of slip-off slopes. There are sweepers along these cut banks.

Boils and surges are infrequent in the Big Salmon River. They are most likely to occur where tributaries such as the North and South Big Salmon River enter. One potential hazard is a whirlpool located at the junction of the Big Salmon and the South Big Salmon Rivers. While it varies in size according to the water volume it will probably be about 0.5 metres deep and 2 metres wide. It can be bypassed by staying on the right shore of the Big Salmon. Other hazards include a couple of log jams that may mean some lining. Remember to stay well clear of these jams. They can swallow a canoe in seconds and should never be used as a landing site.

Below the confluence with the South fork the Semenof Hills border the left of the river, a reminder of the early Russian traders who first explored the Yukon River. At the north end of these hills the Big Salmon flows into the Yukon River.

On the right bank of the river is the abandoned site of Big Salmon, a trading post and Indian village. Old buildings still stand on both sides of the river and can offer protection to boaters caught in foul weather. Canoeists will have to continue on down the Yukon River to Carmacks, another 125 km north. For directions and description see the Yukon River section of this book. Remember to check in at the R.C.M.P. post at Carmacks on the completion of your journey.

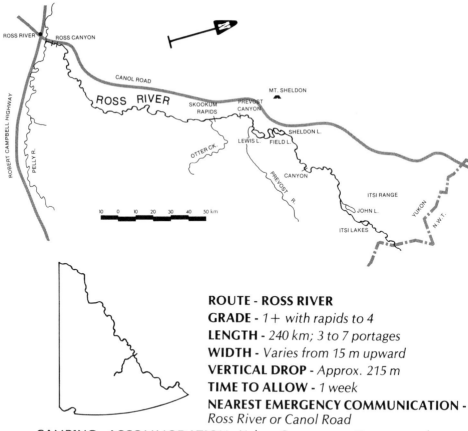

ROUTE - ROSS RIVER
GRADE - *1+ with rapids to 4*
LENGTH - *240 km; 3 to 7 portages*
WIDTH - *Varies from 15 m upward*
VERTICAL DROP - *Approx. 215 m*
TIME TO ALLOW - *1 week*
NEAREST EMERGENCY COMMUNICATION -
Ross River or Canol Road

CAMPING - ACCOMMODATION - *Yukon Government Campground at Ross River; unorganized along river*

MAPS - *N.T.S. 1:250,000 105J Sheldon Lake; 105K Tay River; 105F Quiet Lake*

HAZARDS - *Wilderness, some rapids and canyons*

DIRECTIONS

Fly-in to John Lake on upper part of river, or road access from Canol Road to Sheldon Lake. Take-out at Ross River on Yukon Highway 9.

DESCRIPTION

The Ross River is one of the most attractive of wilderness routes in the Yukon, relatively untouched by logging, mining, or even the fur trade. Canoeists can travel over 200 km of backcountry with just enough white-water and portages to make it interesting. Access too, is not difficult, or expensive. Those wanting to travel as much river as possible may launch in John Lake, reached by float plane. Others wanting to save the cost of a flight, or not wanting to travel the more difficult upper sections, may put-in at Sheldon Lake.

Ross River rises in the Selwyn Mountains and flows from there in a south-westerly direction, through the Boreal Forest Region to the Pelly River. Vegetation along the route ranges from the alpine meadows seen on the mountains near the route's beginning to large stands of mature black and white spruce. The usual willow and alder are found along the river banks. Wildlife likely to be seen includes moose, black bear and beaver as well as small fur bearers. Birds that are common to most rivers like ducks, mergansers, warblers, geese and larger birds of prey will also be seen.

From the route's beginning at John Lake to Sheldon Lake the going can be rough, particularly for the first 20 km. The river here is 10 to 15 metres wide, shallow, and has lots of rocks. This requires a lot of lining and some portaging. The rapids are graded between 3 and 4.

Below this first 20 km section there is an impassable canyon, located 1.5 km past a hairpin turn where the Ross swings to the west. A portage must be made along the right bank for 2 km. Watch closely for this area and try not to run the rapid above the canyon as the take-out will then be much more difficult, having to climb a 10 metre bank.

Below this canyon there is a 30 km run to Sheldon Lake that has only a few sweepers and some gravel bars as obstacles. Directly ahead is Mount Sheldon, dominating the view, and to the south, or left is another unnamed range of mountains.

The route through Sheldon, Field and Lewis Lakes amounts to a total of 16 km of lake paddling that winds through marshland interconnecting this chain of mosquito hatcheries. Just downstream of Lewis Lake the Prevost River flows in from the left.

This next section of river, from the junction to Otter Creek, is swift moving water with a number of rapids. The first rapid is just 5 km downstream and consists of a Grade 3 section followed by Grade 2 in a small canyon. Fifteen km below the Prevost River is Prevost Canyon. This section is marked by 25 to 50 metre canyon walls with shelves and rocks blocking the current. In one place the river flows directly into the rock wall. This canyon should be portaged for 1 km along a trail on the right side.

From Prevost Canyon to Otter Creek, approximately 8 km, there are several sets of rapids. As well as some Grade 2 and 3 there is a difficult Grade 3 spot two km above the creek, and a Grade 4, Skookum Rapids, just 0.5 km above. Scout these carefully and either line or portage if necessary. Skookum can be lined on the right in most water levels.

For the next 112 km the river is a meandering stream with sloughing banks, gravel bars and few difficulties. The Canol Road remains about 5 km away on the right side, separated from the river by an area of marsh and small lakes.

Ten km above the Ross and Pelly confluence the river drops through a canyon with Grade 3 rapids. The Canol Road is nearby. Scout ahead.

On the right bank of the Ross, where it flows into the Pelly River there is an old Indian village and an abandoned trading post. This was once known as Nahanni House, after the Indians who lived at the river's headwaters. There is a ferry and pipeline crossing the river here. Watch for the cable from the ferry and be prepared to duck. Ross River, population about 200, has supplies and accommodation. It is on the Pelly River's right bank about 1 km downstream.

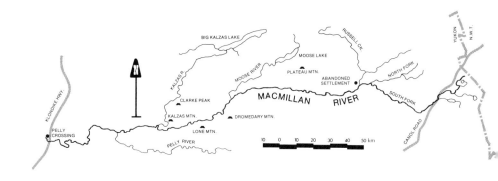

ROUTE - MacMILLAN RIVER - SOUTH MacMILLAN RIVER TO PELLY CROSSING
GRADE - *1 to 2, rapids to 4*
LENGTH - *510 km*
WIDTH - *Up to 150 m*
VERTICAL DROP - *460 m*
TIME TO ALLOW - *2 weeks*
NEAREST EMERGENCY COMMUNICATION - *Ross River, Pelly Crossing*
CAMPING - ACCOMMODATION - *Motel and campground at Ross River; campground at Pelly Crossing; camping unorganized along route*
MAPS - *N.T.S 1:250,000 105J Sheldon Lake; 105K Tay River; 105N Lansing; 105M Mayo; 105L Glenlyon; 115I Carmacks*
HAZARDS - *Remote, rapids, sweepers, log jams*

DIRECTIONS

Road access via Klondike Highway (Hwy 2) to Carmacks, the Robert Camp-bell Highway (Hwy 9) to Ross River and the Canol Road (Hwy 8) to where it crosses the South MacMillan River on a Baillie bridge. Take-out at Pelly Crossing.

DESCRIPTION

The MacMillan River was named by Robert Campbell in 1840 for Chief Factor James McMillan of the H.B.C. He was Campbell's cousin and the man who interested Campbell in the "Great North-West". There is little of historical interest known about the MacMillan River, as little gold was found there; but as a canoe route it is ideal for those who want to experience a wilderness situation, as it is inaccessible to riverboats due to its distance from a fuel supply and to the obstruction caused by log jams.

Both the North and South branches of the MacMillan have their head-waters in the Selwyn Mountains and flow westward through a land of mountains and valleys, becoming one and then entering the Pelly as its largest tributary. The river valley is fairly flat, varying from 1 to 8 km in width.

Access to the North Canol Road from Ross River on the way into the South MacMillan is via a ferry which runs only from 8a.m. to 5p.m. through the summer months.

The route begins in view of the Itsi Range of mountains to the south. The southern slopes of these mountains are headwaters for the Ross River which runs somewhat parallel to the MacMillan for a distance. During the first part of the trip are many unnamed peaks just north of the river. To the south can be seen Mt. Sheldon and Mt. Riddell. After the Riddell River runs in, the South MacMillan is flanked by Mount Selous and the South Fork Range.

For the most part travelling the river is fairly straight forward, with minor surges and cross-currents. Any sweepers or rapids can easily be seen ahead and avoided, with at least one 1 to 2 km portage being necessary in mid summer. There are frequent log jams on side channels. Though there are a few straight stretches on the river, for the most part it consists of continuous meanders.

It is an excellent area to see wildlife. Beaver build their homes in banks along the river and wolves, caribou and moose can also be seen. Both black bear and grizzly are likely to be around when there is salmon in the river. It is interesting to watch for birds such as Bonaparte gulls, Arctic terns, and red-necked loons. Fishing is good for Arctic grayling, whitefish and northern pike. Below Russell Creek salmon may be found.

At the junction of the North and South MacMillan is the site of an old placer mine. About 6 km below this junction, Russell Creek flows in from the north. At the mouth of this creek an abandoned settlement once was a trading post for gold miners on the Russell. Occasionally along the river trappers cabins may be seen, many of which are abandoned and in disrepair.

The river continues meandering westward forming oxbows and islands. Where the river has cut off the oxbows, the water runs a little faster. Suitable camping locations are plentiful on the gravelbars and islands on the river. Though the water may not appear too clear it is potable.

Between the Moose River and the Kalzas River, which both flow in from the north are the Kalzas Range, and beyond the Kalzas River is the Mac-Millan Range. Signs of a former Indian village are evident at the mouth of the Kalzas with graves on one side of the river and abandoned, rotting buildings on the other side.

Below Lone Mountain, the river gradually slows. There continues to be log jams in the side channels but these and gravel bars are less frequent as the Pelly is approached.

After reaching the Pelly, another 70 km brings the river traveller to Pelly Crossing on the Klondike Highway. Tourist facilities are available here, and the Trading Post is one of three in the Yukon operated by an Indian band. Also on the river are Indian fishing camps. For further information on the Pelly, check the Pelly River route.

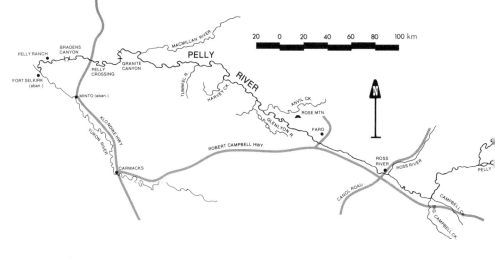

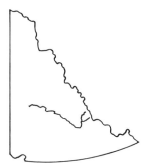

ROUTE - PELLY RIVER
GRADE - *1+, rapids to 2+*
LENGTH - *500 km*
WIDTH - *n/a*
VERTICAL DROP - *Approx. 365 m*
TIME TO ALLOW - *2 weeks*
NEAREST EMERGENCY COMMUNICATION -
Ross River, Faro, Pelly Crossing and Fort Selkirk. Some settlers along the river may be able to lend assistance.
CAMPING - ACCOMMODATION - *Camping unorganized along route; accommodation at Ross River, and Faro*
MAPS - *N.T.S. 1:250,000 105G Finlayson Lake; 105F Quiet Lake; 105K Tay River; 105L Glenlyon; 115I Carmacks*
HAZARDS - *Wilderness, some rapids*

DIRECTIONS
Put-in where Campbell Highway crosses Big Campbell Creek and line or portage to Pelly River, 8 km. Take-out at Pelly Crossing or continue to Fort Selkirk on the Yukon, and then downstream to Dawson City.

DESCRIPTION
The Pelly River canoe route is perhaps the most historic in the Yukon; with the possible exceptions of the Bell-Porcupine or the Yukon itself. It was the Pelly that led the early Hudson's Bay Company traders onto the mainstream of the Yukon, and was the route they used to open up the vast territory. Anyone contemplating the journey should look up at least three books or reports. The first is on the original explorer to visit the area, Robert Campbell. Clifford Wilson has written a book called *Campbell of the Yukon* which gives detail from his journals, and the story of the man. Campbell passed this way in 1843. Years later, in 1887, George Dawson wrote a report on the area for the Geological Survey. His report is listed in the bibliography. Then in 1893 Warburton Pike, adventurer of the north, made his way down the river by a slightly different route, discovering the

Pelly Lakes. His book was titled *Through The Sub-Arctic Forest,* and is now only found in libraries. All of these books will give the traveller a better feeling for the country, and some good route information.

The route, unfortunately, is not quite as wild as when these early voyageurs made their journeys. Modern man has left his marks and scars in a few places, but the route is never-the-less, a fine wilderness experience. For the most part these intrusions do not spoil the atmosphere.

There are two good upstream launching points. The most historic, and probably the easiest, is to take a route similar to Campbell' s. From Watson Lake, Mile 634 on the Alaska Highway, follow the Campbell Highway (Yukon 9), north to Big Campbell Creek, at the 268 km point on this road. Line, paddle and carry 8 km down this stream to the Pelly River. Campbell actually followed a route from Finlayson Lake along Campbell Creek to the same point on the river. It too could be followed, though it is longer and more difficult.

A second access point is Pelly Lakes, 90 km upstream, and reached only by float plane. This section is not described here, but it is relatively simple with one portage at Slate Rapids. For those interested in this longer and more expensive trip, it is described in Pike's book.

The Pelly, like most Yukon Rivers, lies in the Boreal Forest Region where the dominant trees are black and white spruce with some balsam poplar. Along the river are willows and alder, as always. Still remote, it is likely that observant canoeists will see moose, black or grizzly bears, wolves, beaver and many species of waterfowl.

The launching site, where Campbell and Big Campbell Creeks join the Pelly, was the site of Pelly Banks Post, a rather infamous spot in H.B.C. annals where starvation and cannibalism became all too common. It was a posting dreaded by voyageurs. Because of this and the development of the Bell-Porcupine route the post was abandoned in 1850. Later the firm of Taylor & Drury ran a trading post here. Goods were brought down the Yukon and up the Pelly to Ross River by boats, and then on to the post by barges lined up the Pelly. The H.B.C. post was on the left bank of the Pelly, upstream of the creeks.

The first "bad water" of the Pelly is about 40 km downstream at the mouth of the Hoole River. Pike describes it as a formidable rapid with a heavy sea in high water. He managed to run it but shipped a lot of water. There is, or was, a good portage on the north side, the right.

Another 25 km downstream is Hoole Canyon, named by Campbell for Francis Hoole, his interpreter. Pike says this is the worst impediment to navigation on the whole Pelly, and describes it as being impassable for any boat. The current runs into rock walls and there are boulders and whirlpools that also make passage difficult or impossible. There are several small rapids upstream but they can be run. Pike describes the portage of this canyon as being on the left, above a wall of white quartz, just where the stream bends sharply to the northeast. Landing is difficult, but must not be missed. The portage is 18 km long, passing over a wooded hill with a steep descent at the far end. Watch for old skids used by H.B.C. men in

Lapie River Canyon, near Ross River.

dragging boats across. Below the canyon are some small rapids that should be scouted but that can probably be run. Downstream to Ross River canoeing is straight forward with no problems.

The 70 km from Ross River to Faro present no problems to canoeists. Camping is good, the water is fine, and the living can be easy. To the south the Pelly Range can be seen over the sand and clay banks. There are many meanders with uprooted trees, and islands become more numerous.

An old burn marks the approach to Faro, an unattractive town to wilderness buffs, as it is a company town serving Anvil Mine. Limited supplies are available. The town is 1 km from the river.

From Faro to Pelly Crossing has been described as the best 260 km of the river. Mountains dominate much of the view and Fishook Rapids and Granite Canyon break up the meanders with a little white water.

Fishook Rapids appear to be what Campbell called the "Desrivieres", after one of the French Canadians with him. He described it as being 90 miles from Hoole Canyon. The first set, Little Fishook is 3 km upstream of Glenlyon River. The grade 2 rapid is in an S-shaped bend in the river and can be run on the left. At Big Fishook the river flows into a rock wall on the right, and turns left 90 degrees. It too is grade 2.

Below Glenlyon the Tay River flows in from the right, and then 35 km from the rapids the river enters an area that George Dawson described as the Detour. Just beyond where Harvey Creek flows in the river makes a 25 km detour around a ridge. It appears that at one time it flowed straight ahead, then turned and broke through this ridge. The old channel is marked by the Detour Lakes.

Just below the Detour the Tummel River flows in from the south, on the left side. It was named by Robert Campbell for a river in his native Pertshire, Scotland. There is an old trading post at its mouth. Some 35 km downstream the MacMillan River joins the Pelly, adding a large volume of water.

Granite Canyon is 21 km downstream of the MacMillan-Pelly confluence. It is 6.5 km long and confines the river between rock walls 25 metres high, creating three sets of rapids. The first are easily run, being just over grade 1. The second set and third set are 3 km further and have some standing waves and rocks to avoid. A rock in mid-stream divides the river into two channels. Stay to the right. Sternwheelers at one time navigated this canyon as they freighted supplies to Ross River.

Half way from the end of the canyon to Pelly Crossing is the home of the Wilkinson family. Their cabins are on the right side. It shows good river manners to stop and say hello to settlers along the waterway.

A short paddle brings canoes to Pelly Crossing, the spot where the Klondike Highway crosses the river. Those who do not want to paddle the Yukon from Fort Selkirk to Dawson should take out here. There is no accommodation but buses pass once a day and supplies are available. The trading post here is run by the local Indian band.

From Pelly Crossing it is 72 km to the Yukon River, and another 286 km from Fort Selkirk to the next take-out point of Dawson. This will take another 5 or 6 days in total.

The paddle from Pelly Crossing can be accomplished in a day, but more should be allowed for it is an interesting area. Not too far downstream Gull Rocks divide the river into three channels as the 6 metre rocks are passed. The right channel is usually best. Six km below the rocks is Braden's Canyon where strong eddies are present but offer no problems to canoeing.

The canyon is named for a family that have been farming the Pelly since the turn of the century. Originally the Braden farm grew feed for the horses used on the stage line from Dawson to Whitehorse. Now one of the few farms in the Yukon they continue to grow grain as well as raise cattle and vegetables. Their ranch is just 10 km above the Yukon, on the right bank.

Closer to the Yukon, on the left bank, is a wilderness retreat run by John Lammer. Accommodations are sometimes available here.

Fort Selkirk is on the left bank of the Yukon where the Pelly flows in. A description of it is in the Yukon River section of this book. Dawson City, the take-out point is 286 km downstream.

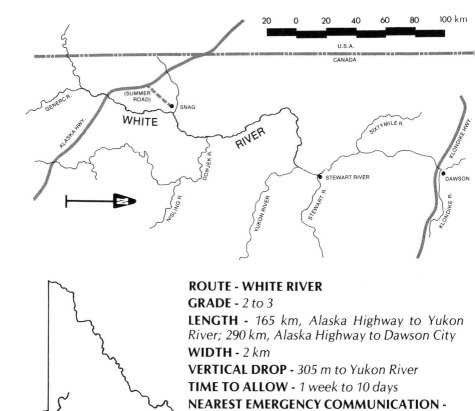

ROUTE - WHITE RIVER
GRADE - *2 to 3*
LENGTH - *165 km, Alaska Highway to Yukon River; 290 km, Alaska Highway to Dawson City*
WIDTH - *2 km*
VERTICAL DROP - *305 m to Yukon River*
TIME TO ALLOW - *1 week to 10 days*
NEAREST EMERGENCY COMMUNICATION - *White River Lodge on Alaska Highway; Dawson City*

CAMPING - ACCOMMODATION - *Unorganized. Camping good on gravel bars. Accommodation and campsite at White River Lodge and in Dawson City*

MAPS - *N.T.S. 1:250,000 115 J,K, Snag; O,N, Stewart or Klondike*

HAZARDS - *Swift water with some rapids, sweepers*

DIRECTIONS

Access to the river is from Mile 1169 on the Alaska Highway or from the abandoned town of Snag, 15 miles downstream, reached by a dirt road. Access is also possible upstream from the Yukon river but only by lining or with a power boat.

DESCRIPTION

"This stream resembles a river of liquid mud of an almost white hue.....The Indians say that the White River rises in glacier-bearing lands, and that it is very swift, and full of rapids along its whole course. So swift is it at its mouth, that as it pours its muddy waters into the rapid Yukon it carries them nearly across that clear blue stream."

So wrote Lieutenant Frederick Schwatka of the United States Army when he passed this point on his journey of 1883. The White had been named by

H.B.C. trader and explorer Robert Campbell in 1851 as he headed downstream on an exploratory trip. Noticing the milky appearance he assumed it to be glaciel silt and named the river for its appearance. In 1891 Schwatka returned to the White River country in search of a pass reputed to be at the head of the river. With him was Charles Hayes, a geologist, who later described the river valley "pursuing its extremely tortuous course among innumerable low islands and bars." They discovered though that the turbidity of the stream was not caused by glacial silt but by an extremely fine deposit of white ash that covered the entire floor of the valley. Walking in it caused them to sink up to a foot in some spots. On this journey they found the area where natives have been mining copper and then crossed via the Scolai Pass to the west side of the mountains.

Later, gold in limited quantities was found on the White and its tributaries, and in the early 1900's it served as a route for miners heading to a gold rush at Chisana, Alaska. Despite earlier warnings by the Indians of canyons, fast water, glaciers and hostile natives the men made their way upstream by poling rafts and small boats, and with small river steamers. A pack train service ran from Coffee Creek to the mining area.

The river is still referred to as a turbulent sometimes dangerous stream but the two canyons are upstream of the highway and the lower section is canoeable. Canoeists should be cautious however, remembering that this is a remote country and once embarked upon there is no help for many kilometres, in fact as far as Dawson City. The river runs at about 8 km with many sections where the narrowing river creates standing waves and large swells. The stream is braided and where channels converge there is usually choppy water with some turbulence. Being glacier fed the water is cold, but undrinkable due to the high volcanic ash content. Carry drinking water. Side channels from the mainstream afford a change of perspective and slower water, but sweepers and log jams must be watched for.

The vistas from the river are generally rather boring and desolate as the valley is very wide, as is the river. The upper reaches offer a view of the Kluane Range, but the lower part is more inclined to offer discarded oil drums and driftwood.

Approximately 24 km from the Alaska Highway Crossing the village of Snag is passed on the right. This can be reached by a dirt road that exits from the Alaska Highway at Mile 1188.6. This abandoned Indian village has the somewhat infamous reputation of having one of the lowest recorded temperatures in Canada, - 62.9 degrees Celsius during the winter of 1946-47.

Below Snag and the confluence of Snag Creek the Donjek River flows in from the right side. This is the largest of three glacier-fed streams that flow into the White. Further downstream the Ladue River flows in from the left. It is named for Joe Ladue, a French-Canadian and early trader in the Yukon Valley. Then the Yukon River is reached and another 135 km of paddling down this river to Dawson City.

Vegetation to be seen along the White includes willow and alder on the gravel bars and some balsam, poplar and spruce. Moose, beaver, bears, geese and ducks are frequently spotted.

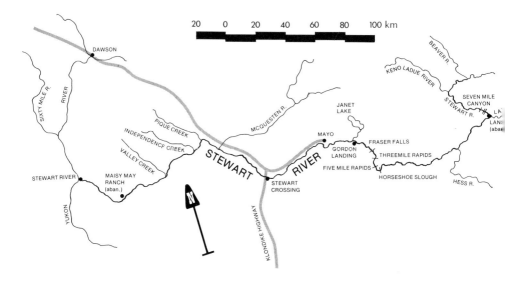

ROUTE - STEWART RIVER - BEAVER RIVER TO DAWSON CITY
GRADE - *1, with rapids to 3*
LENGTH - *580 km*
WIDTH - *75 to 150 m*
VERTICAL DROP - *Approx. 245 m*
TIME TO ALLOW - *2 weeks*
NEAREST EMERGENCY COMMUNICATION - *Mayo, Stewart Crossing, Dawson; highway parallels river between Mayo and McQuesten*
CAMPING - ACCOMMODATION - *Motels at Mayo, Dawson City; public campgrounds at Mayo and Dawson; good camping on gravel bars and river banks; occasional trappers cabins and abandoned settlements for shelter*
MAPS - *N.T.S. 1:250,000 105N Lansing; 105M Mayo; 115P McQuesten; 115O & N(E½) Stewart River; 116B & C(E½) Dawson*
HAZARDS - *Remote, sweepers, rapids*

DIRECTIONS

Road access is via the Klondike Highway (Hwy 3) and then Highway 2 to Mayo; access upstream of this is by air - charter service, available from Mayo. Egress may be at Mayo, Stewart Crossing, McQuesten Emergency Airstrip or at Dawson City on the Yukon River.

DESCRIPTION

The Stewart River, a major tributary of the Yukon, was named by Robert Campbell in 1851 for his hard-working and well-respected assistant, James Green Stewart. The Stewart is one of the relatively easy Yukon rivers to travel by canoe. There is one waterfall which has to be portaged and two or three sets of rapids which must be scouted, and can be portaged if necessary. Otherwise the route is fairly straight forward, passing through scenic countryside varying from rolling hills to canyons and from straight open stretches to large meander bends.

To cover the complete trip discussed here, air access is necessary. However, for those who wish to canoe just that area of the Stewart to which there is road access, a trip from Mayo to Stewart Crossing, 58 km, or from Mayo to McQuesten airstrip, 127 km, is possible. The highway runs parallel to the Stewart for most of this distance. This is probably the least attractive part of the complete route since it lacks the wilderness atmosphere, but it is ideal for those who are not experienced in wilderness travel or for those who have only one or two days to spare.

The route begins in rolling hill country which continues for approximately 50 km, from below the mouth of the Beaver River to Seven Mile Canyon. The view here is limited by the spruce and poplar covered hills on the shores, but upstream glimpses of mountain tops can be seen. Willow, alder and other typical river valley browse are found along the shores. Canoeists will also enjoy the beauty, the smell and possibly even the flavour of wild onions, wild roses and Labrador tea.

The river itself is about 76 metres wide, with a rocky bottom under the slightly silty glacial water. It presents little difficulty to the canoeist, flowing at 5 km/h, with minimal turbulence and no obstructions.

A breach in the rolling terrain occurs where the Keno-Ladue River valley joins the Stewart. The Ladue River is named for Joe Ladue, a Franch-Canadian gold seeker who became a trading partner of Harper and McQuesten. Always an entrepreneur, it was Ladue who chose and staked out the townsite that became Dawson City.

Here mountain views become more prominent with the peaks of Mount Roop and Mount Edwards in the Ladue Range rising to the southwest and Mount Joy in the Lansing Range to the southeast.

Very gradually the river changes. As it widens, meander bends occur more frequently and islands form on the curves. The sandy islands which are treed by spruce and poplar provide good campsite alternatives to the river banks - river water is drinkable, driftwood is available for firewood and river breezes keep mosquitoes to a bearable level.

Minor hazards and obstructions in the river, such as sandbars, sweepers and riffles, can be easily recognized and avoided. As Seven Mile Canyon is approached occasional rapids are formed by bedrock ledges but these too can be skirted.

Rolling hills change to rocky shores and then to rock walls, and the river narrows into a single channel as Seven Mile Canyon begins. The canyon walls reach to 45 metres and are topped by spruce. Now and then the bank sloughs off to form a bench, sometimes treed, which make good stopping places or campsites.

There are many surges and small whirlpools in the canyon, and rapids where bedrock ledges jut into the river. The maximum drop caused by the ledges appears to be about 3 decimetres. However the canyon can be navigated and the rapids and ledges avoided. For example, at the beginning of the canyon, rapids caused by a ledge on the right side of the river can be bypassed on the left. Throughout the canyon back eddies are useful for resting or stopping.

A short distance below the mouth of Seven Mile Canyon, the Lansing River flows in from the Hess Mountains to the east. Situated on its north bank is the abandoned settlement of Lansing. It was set up as a trading post for prospectors along the Stewart in the late 1800's. Now only a few deteriorating buildings remain.

For the 100 km from Lansing to Five Mile Rapids the Stewart heads in a southwesterly direction. Long straight stretches of river bordered by treed, hilly landscape are interspersed with large meander bends and sloughed off banks up to 100 metres high. Along the meanders are sandbars, islands and occasional sweepers. The river widens over this area from 100 to 150 metres, continuing its flow of about 5 km/h. The canoeist must watch for sandbars and sweepers along the bends of the river.

About 42 miles past Lansing the Hess River flows in from the east. Below there, along the meander bends, occasional oxbows and sloughs have formed. Other interesting features along this section of the river are several trappers cabins in varying stages of disrepair.

Five Mile Rapids marks the beginning of the only difficult areas of water on the river. They run for 8 km through two sets of rapids to Fraser Falls. Both rapids can usually be run but must first be scouted and assessed. Fraser Falls must be portaged.

Check out Five Mile Rapids by stopping on the right side on a gravel bar above the rapids and climbing a trail overlooking the river. The grade 2 to 3 rapid may be run down the centre chute by experienced canoeists in some water levels, but an easier route is along the right bank close to shore. If preferred, the canoe can be lined along the left shore or portaged on either the left or right side.

After a quiet stretch of about 3 km, Three Mile Rapid is approached. It can be scouted by keeping to the right and landing in a bay above the rapids. Rated as Grade 3 the river is divided into two chutes by a large rock. The left chute may be run by experienced canoeists in higher water levels; the right side is easier in lower levels. Be aware of the standing waves of up to 1 metre and the strong back eddy caused by the large rock. The rapid may be portaged on the right.

Below Three Mile Rapid the river runs fairly quietly for about 4.8 km, with only a few riffles caused by rock ledges. Then the water speed increases as Fraser Falls is approached. Take-out on the left bank to follow the portage along an old coach road which leads to a couple of abandoned buildings, all that is left of the settlement of Fraser Falls. It is possible to view the falls by crossing the Stewart below the falls and climbing back up the right bank. The river drops about 8 metres in half a kilometre, more of a cascade than a sharp falls. The falls are probably named for John Fraser, one of the early miners to work the Stewart bars.

From Fraser Falls, the narrow canyon quickly opens into a wide flat river valley, through which the water course is fairly straight with a few meanders and sloughing banks toward Mayo. The water volume increases with the waters from many creeks, mostly unnamed, that enter from both sides of the river, but the river slows to 3 to 5 km/h and headwinds may impede progress. The occasional cabins seen along shore are mostly in poor repair.

For those interested in hiking or fishing, a trail leads from Gordon Landing 5 km to the headwaters of Janet Creek in Janet Lake. The clear cold waters are a good place to fish for Arctic grayling. Gordon Landing once boasted a population of 200 residents, but lost out to the rival community of Mayo Landing.

Formerly the river settlement of Mayo Landing, Mayo is now the supply centre for a region rich in minerals, and especially noted as one of the richest silver mining regions in Canada. It provides welcome respite to the canoeists, with a variety of facilities and supplies available, including a hospital, R.C.M.P., grocery store and public campground. Mayo takes its name from Albert H. Mayo, an ex circus acrobat who was a partner of McQuesten when he first came to the Yukon in 1873.

From Mayo to McQuesten airstrip, a distance of 127 km, a road (Highways 2 and 3) closely follows the river. The water course continues to alternate between relatively straight stretches and meanders and sloughs. It is bordered by the rolling hillsides, cut banks, spruce and poplar typical of the area, and, occasionally, mountains as the meanders extend to the valley limits. A disadvantage of travelling in a more populated area as this is that the water is more polluted. Water should be taken from the frequent clear streams entering the Stewart.

At Stewart Crossing, where the Klondike Highway crosses the Stewart River, a ferry has been replaced by a bridge. A restaurant-lodge is located here as well.

Moose Creek is another good place to fish for Arctic grayling. There is a public campground about 1 km up Moose Creek, where the highway crosses. Another bridge and crossing, unseen from the Stewart, is upstream of the Stewart-McQuesten junction. McQuesten is named for LeRoy Napoleon (Jack) McQuesten, the famed trader whose fortune lay in selling supplies to gold miners. He set up many trading posts, including the one at Stewart River, at the Yukon-Stewart junction.

The McQuesten Airstrip, 5 km downstream of the McQuesten River is used only in emergencies. Across the river from the airstrip is Steamboat Bar, one of the earliest bars worked for gold, and a productive one. It was said to have been "a regular thing for each rocker to clear up.....to $300 per day."

The river heads westward again, away from the highway, meandering 130 km to its junction with the Yukon. There are many islands and bars along the way. Some of the side channels are blocked with debris. Most of the bars and creeks were worked by early gold miners. Old cabins can still be found as well as an abandoned wagon road following Scroggie Creek along the Stewart and up Black Hills Creek. Gold was found in these creeks until long after the main Klondike rush.

At Maisy May Creek there is a farm which once provided hay for the Whitehorse to Dawson stagecoach line. Some of the trappers cabins are still in use; many are protected by the Yukon Territorial Government. Watch for signs of beaver.

As the volume of the Stewart gets larger the current increases to 6 to 10 km/h. Again canoeists must be on the lookout for sandbars, sweepers and riffles, but should have no problems.

The first prospectors who worked on Stewart bars with encouraging results were four men from Juneau in 1883. By the summer of 1886 there were around a hundred miners in the area, most of whom were doing well. McQuesten and Harper had established a post at the mouth of the Stewart and a small community was formed called Stewart River. But when gold was found on the Klondike interest in the Stewart faded. In later years however, some miners came back to the Stewart and continued to find gold on some of its tributaries.

Nearing the mouth of the Stewart it is a good idea to swing to the left channel, entering the Yukon as far upstream as possible. This will lead you past the Buriens small store on Stewart Island. They have a few basic supplies and refreshments for sale as well as a small museum, and a lot of Yukon history stored in their memories.

The completion of this route is accomplished by paddling the Yukon 112 km to Dawson City, which will take 1 to 2 days of paddling. The Sixtymile River makes a good overnight stop. Further information on this section can be found in the Yukon River route description.

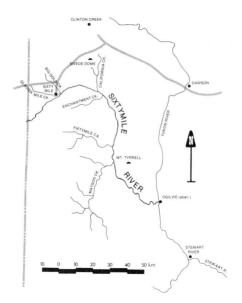

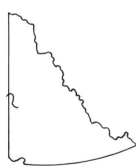

ROUTE - SIXTYMILE RIVER - GLACIER CREEK TO DAWSON CITY

GRADE - *2 except for rapids*

LENGTH - *240 km*

WIDTH - *15 to 45 m*

VERTICAL DROP - *430 m*

TIME TO ALLOW - *6 days*

NEAREST EMERGENCY COMMUNICATION - *Customs office on the Yukon-Alaska border, Dawson City*

CAMPING - ACCOMMODATION - *Motels and campgrounds at Dawson City; along the route good camping on sandbars at mouths of tributary creeks*

MAPS - *N.T.S. 1:250,000 116B-116C(E½) Dawson; 1150-115N(E½) Stewart River*

HAZARDS - *Sandbars, boulders, sweepers and rapids*

DIRECTIONS

Road access is via the Klondike Highway (Hwy 3); approximately 80 km west of Dawson City, a rough side road heads south to the abandoned settlement of Sixtymile on Glacier Creek. This is about 1.5 km above the junction of Glacier Creek with the Sixtymile River. Take-out is at Dawson City.

DESCRIPTION

The Sixtymile River and several other rivers in the area took their names from their distances from Fort Reliance the Sixtymile being located 60 miles upstream. The river is suitable for experienced canoeists but requires a considerable amount of portaging, lining and hauling on the first part of the route where shallow water and obstacles make it unnavigable for the most part. As the river increases in volume, less lining and hauling are required.

The river itself rises just inside the Alaskan border, flowing east and south into the Yukon River, about 36 km north of the mouth of the Stewart River. The length of the river is almost twice the length of the valley it has created, as river winds and twists continuously over its complete course. The average drop is 2 m/km.

Historically the Sixtymile was one of the many gold creeks prior to the Klondike gold discovery, and Ogilvie Post across from its mouth was a stopping place for the miners heading to the Klondike. Remnants of the past can still be seen along the river, such as the remains of the miners cabins, tailings, and even a dredge at the former settlement of Sixtymile.

The access road from the Klondike Highway to Sixtymile is best suited to four wheel drive vehicles. From here the portaging, lining and hauling begin, down to the mouth of Glacier Creek and along as far as California Creek. The river is narrow, and shallow flowing over cobble beds with frequent bars and boulders. Canoeists are advised to have shoes suitable to protect feet while walking along the river bed and to have a good canoe repair kit along.

The river valley is fairly wide and flat with terraced riversides and occasional rock walls, sometimes as high as 45 metres. Bordering the valley are rounded hills. Vegetation along most of the river is typical of the Boreal Forest Region, with white and black spruce, alder and willow. The wildlife is similar to that along most other Yukon rivers, with bears, moose and water fowl most commonly seen.

From California Creek to Fiftymile Creek, the increase in water volume is noticeable. There are still many bars, boulders and sweepers requiring careful navigation and some lining and hauling. Bars at the creek mouths are good for camping and these spots also provide good fishing for Arctic grayling.

Below Fiftymile Creek the going is easier. Rapids are fairly common, but not difficult to navigate. The only obstructions that may cause a problem are sweepers. The river widens considerably below Tenmile Creek to about 45 metres. There is a good camping area close to the mouth of the Sixtymile. Swimming here is more pleasant than in the colder, siltier Yukon and fishing is good for northern pike and whitefish.

Across from the mouth of the Sixtymile, is Sixtymile Island on which was located Ogilvie Post. The settlement was named for William Ogilvie, the government surveyor who helped establish the boundary between Alaska and the Yukon. The trader who opened this post was Joseph Ladue who served the needs of gold miners in the area. When gold was discovered on the Klondike, Ladue moved his trading post and sawmill from here to the site that was to become Dawson City. The first post office in the Yukon was established at Ogilvie in 1894. Now only a few decaying log cabins are left to mark this historic post.

The remaining 80 km of this route are on the Yukon River down to Dawson City.

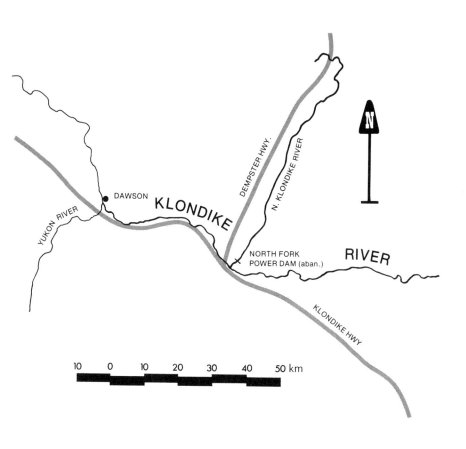

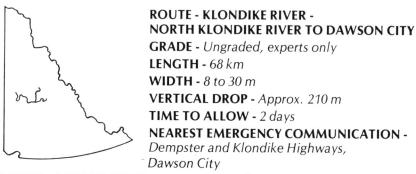

**ROUTE - KLONDIKE RIVER -
NORTH KLONDIKE RIVER TO DAWSON CITY**
GRADE - *Ungraded, experts only*
LENGTH - *68 km*
WIDTH - *8 to 30 m*
VERTICAL DROP - *Approx. 210 m*
TIME TO ALLOW - *2 days*
NEAREST EMERGENCY COMMUNICATION -
*Dempster and Klondike Highways,
Dawson City*

CAMPING - ACCOMMODATION - *Motels and campgrounds at Dawson City; unorganized camping along the route, though sites may be difficult to find on the North Klondike*

MAPS - *N.T.S. 1:250,000 116B-116C(E½) Dawson; 1150 & N(E½) Stewart River*

HAZARDS - *Sweepers*

DIRECTIONS

Road access is via the Klondike Highway (Hwy 3) and then the Dempster Highway (Hwy 11); about 11 km north of the Highway 3 and 11 junction, an old side road to the right leads to the North Klondike River. Take-out at Dawson City.

DESCRIPTION

The Klondike gained renown as the site of the richest and most famous of all gold rushes after gold was discovered on Bonanza Creek, one of its tributaries, in 1897. This is the same river that Frederick Schwatka referred to as the Deer River, so named for the caribou that passed by during their migration. It was also called the Trundeck by Jack McQuesten, from which it evolved to Trondiuck and Klondike through various pronunciations. According to William Ogilvie, Trondiuck meant "hammer-water", referring to the hammering into the river bed of stakes on the fish traps used by the Indians at the mouth of the river to catch salmon. Through the years this valley was the source of an estimated $300 million.

Canoeing on the Klondike River provides an insight into this historic region and the effect of man on the environment. The river is suitable only for experienced canoeists. However it is neither a long nor a remote route, as many of the other Yukon routes are, for the Dempster and Klondike Highways parallel the North Klondike and Klondike Rivers respectively. There is only one portage required.

The river begins in the Ogilvie Mountains, with the North Klondike running south and joining the Klondike flowing from the east. Together they continue westward to the junction of the Klondike with the Yukon at Dawson City.'The surrounding country is part of the Boreal Forest Region, which is well treed with black and white spruce, alder and willow. The area generally has little precipitation through the summer months. Watch for beaver, moose and waterfowl along the river.

The route description begins at a point about 16 km up the North Klondike River. The water is fairly shallow being less than a metre in depth and about 8 metres wide in mid summer. There are small riffles as the water flows swiftly over the rocky bottom. Sloughing river banks cause some back eddies and result in many sweepers to be avoided. Some lining may be necessary.

About half way to the North Klondike-Klondike junction the old North Fork power dam is reached. The dam which is no longer in use can be by-passed by a 200 metre portage. The North Klondike now runs through the dam and may become canoeable sometimes in high water.

After about 16 km, the Klondike River is reached. This river is about four times wider than the North Klondike, and shallow water and sweepers are no longer a problem. Below Rock Creek the river becomes braided. The course of the river will be seen to have been changed by the dredging operations of long ago, causing riffles and rapid sections. During the gold rush miners extracted gold using rockers, hydraulicking methods and then dredges. Along the Klondike River can still be seen the tailings and the remains of equipment such as dredges which was used and then

Dawson City - 1900, Yukon Archives Photo.

abandoned. Over the last 13 km before the Yukon is reached, the tailings have eliminated all the plant life. Behind are the Moosehide Hills to the north and the Klondike Hills to the south.

It is extimated that the Klondike and its tributaries yielded more than $300 million in gold. Small creeks like the Hunker and Bear were said to have produced more than a million dollars apiece, and the Bonanza, where the first strikes were made, produced more than three million. Hunker Creek, named for a miner, Andrew Hunker, was Bob Henderson's Gold Bottom Creek, and it was on this tributary he was working when the Bonanza and Klondike were being staked, causing him to miss out on the big strikes. Gold was really discovered on the Bonanza as a result of Henderson telling George Carmacks, Skookum Jim and Tagish Charlie of gold in the area; however the three did not return the favor to Henderson and failed to let him know of their own finds which triggered the Klondike Gold Rush.

Arctic grayling may be caught in the Klondike and North Klondike, with some northern pike and whitefish near the Klondike mouth. There are also salmon at the mouth, where the Indians used to have a fish camp and catch salmon in traps.

The site of Dawson City was chosen by Joseph Ladue to serve the miners on the Klondike. It was surveyed by William Ogilvie and named by him for his superior, geologist George Mercer Dawson. Originally laid out for 30,000, the present population is less than 1000. The largest city in Canada west of Winnipeg in 1900, Dawson City almost became a ghost town. Now it is experiencing a comeback as a tourist town and as a supply centre for northern construction and development. Some of the old buildings are also being restored. Discovery Day is now a Yukon holiday to celebrate the Klondike discovery of August 17, 1897.

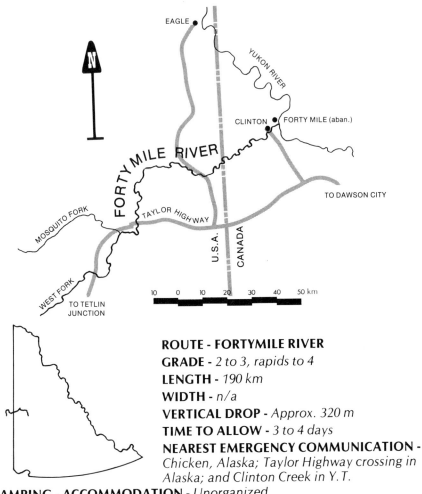

ROUTE - FORTYMILE RIVER
GRADE - *2 to 3, rapids to 4*
LENGTH - *190 km*
WIDTH - *n/a*
VERTICAL DROP - *Approx. 320 m*
TIME TO ALLOW - *3 to 4 days*
NEAREST EMERGENCY COMMUNICATION - *Chicken, Alaska; Taylor Highway crossing in Alaska; and Clinton Creek in Y.T.*
CAMPING - ACCOMMODATION - *Unorganized*
MAPS - *N.T.S. 1:250,000 116B-116C(E½) Dawson*
HAZARDS - *Rapids*

DIRECTIONS

Put-in at one of the access points in Alaska, from Klondike Loop road, and take-out at Clinton Creek, Y.T.

DESCRIPTION

Although the better part of this route lies in Alaska, Yukon paddlers may be attracted by its exciting water and reputation as a lineal museum of the goldrush.

This river is best suited to experienced paddlers with a fair amount of whitewater or river paddling. Open canoes can make the run but may have to portage some rapids. It is excellent for inflatables. As all four starting points are in Alaska be sure to check with Canadian customs regarding re-entry before making the trip.

The highest access point is at Mile 128 on the Taylor Highway from Dawson to Tetlin Junction. This is the West Fort Bridge. Access point 2 is 32 km downstream at the Chicken Creek bridge at the settlement of Chicken. Chicken is named for the ptarmigan often seen in this area. Access point 3 is at Mile 101 of the Taylor Highway at the South Fort bridge. The lowest point of access is from the Eagle road which leaves the Taylor Highway just west of the border between Yukon and Alaska.

Although the majority of the river is not too difficult there are some rapids which reach grade 3 or 4, all of which should be scouted. The first 50 km are fast, dropping 4.5 metres per km. Below Chicken the river widens and the current slows down. However there are six rapids that should be watched for. The first is 8 km below the Chicken bridge; the second just below the junction with the North Fork; the third, 23 km upstream from the highway bridge at Mile 101; the fourth and fifth, Deadman Riffle and Eldon Landing Rapids are close to the Alaska-Yukon border; the final one, though unnamed, is the worst. It forms two sections and should be lined along the left bank during highwater, or if it is chancey for your skills.

The easiest take-out on the Fortymile River is at Clinton Creek, an asbestos mine run by Cassiar Asbestos Corporation. There are few services here as it is a company town. Access to the town is at Mile 38 of the Taylor Highway or Klondike Loop road. Continuing down the river 5 km will bring you to the old settlement of Forty Mile, established in 1887 by McQuesten and Harper. The next point of egress though would then be Eagle, Alaska, an additional 88 km downstream.

One of the attractions of this route is that it gives one a reason to travel the "Top of the World Highway". For most of the journey from Dawson the highway meanders like a river around and across the tops of the mountains, always trying to keep its contour line the same, usually far above timber line.

The river was named for its distance from Fort Reliance, just downstream of Dawson City. Schwatka, the American explorer who drifted down the Yukon called the stream the Cone-Hill River for a hill in the centre of the valley. Fortunately his name did not stick.

By 1894 the settlement at the mouth of the gold stream was sizable and progressing quickly. There were 150 log cabins, about 6 good sized houses and a warehouse belonging to McQuesten and Harper. Bishop Bompas had built a mission on an island near the mouth, which also held the Indian village. A kilometre or so downstream was Fort Cudahy, some cabins and a post of the North American Transportation and Trading Company. The following year Fort Constantine was built here, the first post of the North West Mounted Police in the Yukon Territories.

Only one year later gold was found on the Klondike river and the city of Dawson began, drawing the population and commerce of Fortymile up-river. In 1901 Bishop Bompas left the deserted settlement for Carcross. He was the last to go. Today all that remains is his church, a few cabins and a store, now used as an overnight stop for river travellers.

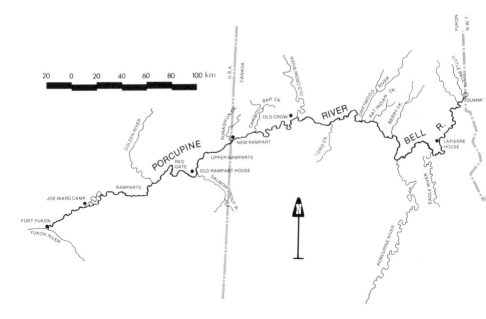

ROUTE - BELL-PORCUPINE RIVERS
GRADE - *2*
LENGTH - *250 km - Summit Lake to Old Crow Y.T.; 820 km - Summit Lake to Fort Yukon, Alaska*
WIDTH - *3 decimetres to 250 m*
VERTICAL DROP - *180 m to Alaska border*
TIME TO ALLOW - *3 weeks to Fort Yukon*
NEAREST EMERGENCY COMMUNICATION - *Old Crow and Fort Yukon*

CAMPING - ACCOMMODATION - *Unorganized. Infrequent sites on the Bell and Upper Porcupine because of high banks*

MAPS - *N.T.S. 1:250,000 116P Bell River; 116ON Old Crow; U.S. Army Corps of Engineers Q501 series; NQ7, 8-1 Coleen, Alaska; NQ7, 8-5 Black River, Alaska; NQ5, 6-8 Fort Yukon, Alaska*

HAZARDS - *Remote; rapid changes in water level (from 1 to 2m) overnight; flooding may occur*

DIRECTIONS

Access by float plane to Summit Lake at 67 42.5' N. Lat., 136 28' W. Long.; Access also possible by paddling upstream from Aklavik N.W.T. into the Rat River and McDougall Pass.

DESCRIPTION

This route is unique in Canada for here is a canoe route that offers an opportunity to follow an historic trading route of the Hudson's Bay

Company and one that lies entirely north of the Arctic circle and the southern limit of permafrost. The rivers cut through tundra that is broken only by riverbank trees. The weather remains cool all summer and in the late summer and fall migrating caribou cross the rivers as they surge south in a living carpet to their southern wintering grounds. This is truly a northern journey.

From an historical aspect this is an attractive route for it follows the trails of the native peoples and the route used by the Hudson's Bay Company to connect Fort Simpson with the post of Lapierre on the Bell River, Rampart House on the Porcupine River and Fort "Youcon" on the Yukon River. McDougall Pass in the Richardson Mountains was the only portage between the Mackenzie and Yukon River systems, and the lowest pass in the mountain ranges that form the spine of the North American continent, only 762 metres in elevation. In later years the trails were used by Klondikers heading for the Yukon goldfields, who were also attracted by the low elevation of the pass. Today aircraft wing across the old fur trade route, often landing on Summit Lake to refuel from gasoline caches.

The route has two major accesses. The first is to fly into Summit Lake in McDougall Pass, on the headwaters of the Little Bell River, by float plane. From here the paddling is all downstream. A second access is from the Mackenzie system and entails starting at Aklavik, Inuvik or Fort McPherson and going up the Rat River by canoe to the pass. Eric Morse, in his excellent book *Fur Trade Canoe Routes of Canada / Then and Now,* describes this latter route as one of the most physically challenging of fur trade routes left today. It takes nine days to line, pole and wade up the cold Rat River to the pass. Then a 1 km portage leads to Summit Lake, where others have flown in to begin the trip.

This route was first travelled for the Hudson's Bay Company by John Bell, in 1839. On an exploratory trip of the Peel River he had talked to Indians who told him that the Rat River led west to the mountains where a short portage led to another great river and where at the height of land he would find an annual meeting of Indians gathered to trade. After bartering with the Indians at the pass Bell returned to Fort Good Hope for the winter.

In 1842 he returned to explore the river that is now named for him, following it and the Porcupine downstream to what is now the area of the international border. In 1844 he continued further down the Porcupine to a broad river which he heard the natives call the "Youcon". At this point, 3 years later, Fort Yukon was established.

In the meantime a satellite post of Fort McPherson, sometimes called Peel's River Post, had been built west of McDougall Pass on the Bell River. This was called Lapierre House, and is still in evidence today.

Having arrived at Summit Lake canoeists may want to spend a couple of days hiking in the beautiful Richardson Mountains. Photographers will enjoy the panoramas of the Rat River Valley, McDougall Pass, the Little Bell River valley and the Richardson Mountains. While there is excellent camping on the mossy banks of the lake, firewood is scarce and a small stove would be useful. Do not disturb the fuel caches seen along the shore.

One of the most difficult sections of the journey must be hurdled right at the beginning. A small creek exits from the lake at the western end, but its width averages between 3 and 9 decimetres. In addition it is 3 to 5 metres below the valley floor, and is heavily overgrown with alder and willow. In August this creek will be dry. The best water levels occur in June and July. Canoeists who elect to try this route must be prepared for a great deal of plowing through mud and chopping of undergrowth as the creek is lined and waded down. The alternative is a 1 km portage from Summit Lake to the Little Bell River.

The small creek from Summit Lake enters the Little Bell River about 13 km upstream from the Bell River. The route is twisting, with many snags and sweepers. Steep undercut mud banks make campsites difficult to find. At the mouth of the river, where it flows into the Bell, there are several small rapids where the water flows over sharp rocks. If the water level is high these may be easily run, but if it is low they should be lined.

The Bell River meanders slowly and laboriously down to the Porcupine with no navigational hazards. High banks continue to make campsites difficult to find. Moose are often seen as well as various ducks and geese. About half way to the Porcupine, where the river begins to widen, the remains of Lapierre House will be seen on the right bank. Two old cabins and a cache are all that remain of this once important post. It was at this post that Alexander Murray left his new bride while he went further west to build Fort Yukon in 1847. They did not see each other for a year, during which time Mrs. Murray give birth to a daughter Helen, the first white child to be born in what is now the Yukon Territory. From Lapierre House west Murray used a York boat which had been built at the post.

Below the "small house" the Rock and then the Eagle River flow in from the left and south. From the mouth of the Eagle River it is another 50 km to the Porcupine.

It was on this Eagle River which canoeists are now passing that the trail ended for Albert Johnson, the "Mad Trapper of Rat River." The manhunt for Johnson began in December of 1931, on the east side of the Richardson mountains when Indians reported to the R.C.M.P. a trapper who was trying to take over their trap lines and who constantly threatened them. On the 28th officers from the Arctic Red River Post visited his fortified cabin on the Rat River, but he would not let them enter. On the next visit he shot one of them. Reinforced with more men the R.C.M.P. tried to shoot it out, but failed. Even several dynamite blasts failed to budge the trapper. When they returned to Aklavik for supplies Johnson shouldered his pack and guns and headed west in an attempt to reach Alaska. During his six week flight across the mountains in the dead of an Arctic winter he shot and killed Constable Millen of the R.C.M.P. Circling, zig-zaging and travelling behind caribou herds to hide his tracks he managed to stay ahead of his pursuers for weeks. Finally, tired and worn-out from constant travel he stumbled down the banks of the Eagle river, into two posses. One was headed south from Lapierre House and the other had caught up to his tracks and came from the south. In a final desperate attempt not to be taken he tried to shoot it out, wounding two men. Finally he was surrounded and shot on a large bend of the river as he crouched behind a

Old Crow.

river bank rock. It was Feb. 17th, 1931. Who Albert Johnson was remains a mystery to this day.

Once on the Porcupine, named for the abundance of these animals, there is 70 km of paddling on a stream that is generally broad and slow, with little current and long straight sections. York boats often ran aground along here. The banks are low and muddy with occasional views of the high but bald mountains to the north. The occasional groves of large spruce that interrupt the lines of willow and alder along the shore make the best campsites. Old cabins can often be seen along the shore, some more or less habitable. Below Driftwood River the current of the river quickens and the country becomes more hilly. The Old Crow range can be seen to the north.

The settlement of Old Crow is located on the northwest bank of the Old Crow and Porcupine confluence, that is the right bank of each river. At this native settlement there is a R.C.M.P. detachment and a store where supplies may be replenished. Air service to other Yukon points makes this a possible egress point for canoeists.

The increased speed of the river now makes it possible to make 80 to 95 km per day. One good stopping point, a short days journey from Old Crow, is on the left bank about 56 km below the village. There is an excellent cabin here at last report.

From Old Crow to Caribou Bar Creek the river meanders between high bluffs and then below Caribou Bar Creek begins to narrow to the Ramparts. This term for the canyon like walls was used by the early explorers and traders that used the route, including Murray who remarked that the river became narrow and the current much stronger between the rocky hills and precipices. At one point he described a narrows called the "Carribeaux Leap" where the channel was said to be so narrow that one could leap across it. The current is swift through the Ramparts and there are a few chutes. This last for about 80 km. Campsites are easily found.

New Ramparts House, 10 km below Caribou Bar is another good spot for the photographer. This abandoned but interesting site was built by the Hudson's Bay Company when the survey of 1891 showed their Ramparts House to be in the U.S.A.'s Alaska. It was abandoned long ago. Sunagun Creek enters from the north and the mouth of it marks the international border.

Ramparts House, several kilometres below the boundary, was built in 1869 by the Hudson's Bay Company when the Americans decided to evict them from Fort Yukon as illegal traders on foreign soil, something the H.B.C. had chosen to ignore for many profitable years. The site of the post is the mouth of the Salmon Trout River. Firshermen are advised to detour up the river for 1.5 km to a canyon where good fishing for grayling can be had.

Red Gate, 10 km below Old Ramparts House, marks the end of the Upper Ramparts of the Porcupine. Below here the surrounding land becomes flat, and the river is slower with more frequent islands. Eight kilometres below Red Gate is the recently abandoned site of Canyon village, a native settlement.

About 65 km below the Upper Ramparts the Lower Ramparts begin, though they are not as spectacular as the upper section. The river moves slowly between the 100 metre canyon walls. Downstream of the Lower Ramparts the Porcupine enters the Yukon River Flats. For close to 200 km the river wanders through sloughs and meander bends, over shallow gravel bars and around cut banks. If the water level is sufficiently high several shortcuts may be taken. Shorter and narrower than the main channel these shortcuts offer better chances of seeing wildlife. There are many cabins through this section. Joe Ward Camp and Shuman House are on the right bank at the mouth of a creek but are boarded up, at last report.

Fort Yukon, the terminus of this route, lies 3.5 km above the confluence of the Porcupine and Yukon Rivers. The Yukon current is too strong to paddle against and the portage is hard to find. Stand on the upper end of the gravel bar on the upper end of Homebrew Island. Look across at the south, or left bank of the river to where there are three distinct breaks in the spruce. The lowest and widest marks the head of the trail. Willows in this gap and a lowering in the cutbank mark where the Porcupine sometimes overflows. The trail starts in the spruce just above the willows. Fort Yukon is on the right bank of the Yukon on Hospital Lake, a slough once part of the Porcupine. The 300 metre portage leads to this slough. Leave your gear at the airstrip dock and hitch a ride into town. Remember you are now in the United States of America.

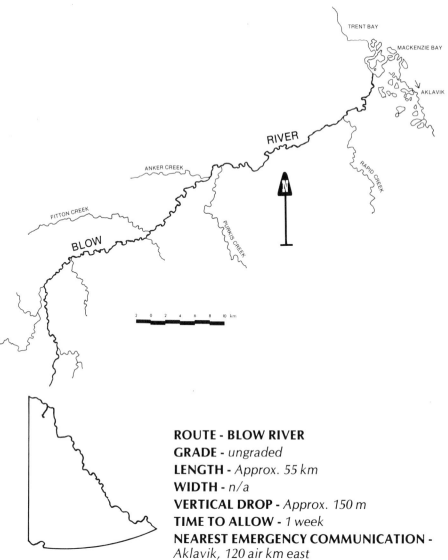

ROUTE - BLOW RIVER
GRADE - *ungraded*
LENGTH - *Approx. 55 km*
WIDTH - *n/a*
VERTICAL DROP - *Approx. 150 m*
TIME TO ALLOW - *1 week*
NEAREST EMERGENCY COMMUNICATION -
Aklavik, 120 air km east
CAMPING - ACCOMMODATION - *Unorganized*
MAPS - *N.T.S. 1:250,000 117A Blow River*
HAZARDS - *Uncharted route, extremely remote, difficult access*

DIRECTIONS

Aircraft to headwaters or line and carry upstream from the Arctic Ocean; aircraft from Inuvik or Aklavik.

DESCRIPTION

No voyageur ever needs to feel that they have canoed all the Yukon waters, for whenever you may think they are all done there will still be rivers like the Blow. This is wilderness in the extreme, a land unequalled in few parts of the world. It is almost certain that you will see no one during the whole trip.

Information on this river is almost non-existent, except that it is, or has been paddled. Access appears to be a problem. An approach could be made upstream by landing at Shingle Point Landing Ground on Trent Bay, in Mackenzie Bay. Aircraft could be chartered out of Aklavik or Inuvik. There does not appear to be any suitable upstream landing points for aircraft. Another alternative would be to follow the example of some Alaskan paddlers who when stymied by lack of access decided to parachute with folded kayaks into the headwaters of their route.

The river begins in the valley between the Richardson and the Barn Mountain Ranges and flows north out of the mountains, through tundra and across the Arctic Coastal Plain. There are of course no trees here so stoves will have to be taken, and there is virtually no emergency assistance. A portable radio of some kind might be advisable or an air check. The route should of course be surveyed from the air prior to actually making the journey.

The route would end in Trent Bay and pickup would be from Shingle Point Landing Ground. Alternatives would be to paddle approximately 160 km west to Aklavik, difficult to find in the Mackenzie Delta, or to paddle west to Herschel Island, where there is usually a summer crew of government people. Herschel Island is 130 km west with ocean paddling all the way.

This is not a route for the inexperienced or easily discouraged paddler. A final note: This is the arctic. Travel with clothing and rations suitable to survive a long storm and cold spell. There is no one to help you out there.

A herd of Barren-Ground Caribou north of Old Crow, Yukon Tourism & Information Photo.

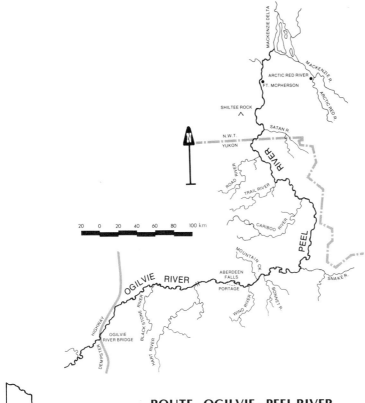

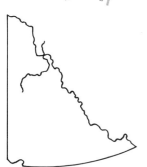

ROUTE - OGILVIE - PEEL RIVER
GRADE - *1+, rapids 3 to 6*
LENGTH - *700 km; 2+ portages*
WIDTH - *35 m to 1 km*
VERTICAL DROP - *750 m*
TIME TO ALLOW - *15 days to Fort McPherson; 3 weeks to Inuvik*
NEAREST EMERGENCY COMMUNICATION - *Dempster Highway; Fort McPherson, Inuvik*
CAMPING - ACCOMMODATION - *Unorganized*
MAPS - *N.T.S. 1:250,000 116F,G Ogilvie River; 116H Hart River, 106E Wind River; 106K Martin House; 106L Trail River; 106M Fort McPherson*
HAZARDS - *Remote, many difficult rapids.*

DIRECTIONS
Access at Mile 123 of Dempster Highway, or further along Highway. Egress at Fort McPherson, or preferably Inuvik.

DESCRIPTION
A canoe journey down the Ogilvie-Peel system is a major undertaking, not to be attempted except by the experienced white-water, wilderness paddler. Of the total 700 km, about 450 km is completely remote from civilization and any kind of emergency assistance. This is a wild river, with many rapids, sections that have to be lined and some portages, one of which is over 8 km in length. The trip must be planned carefully with sup-

plies for at least three weeks and emergency rations for longer. Gear should be carefully stowed and secured, and canoes should be fitted with spray covers.

The Pelly was first found by the H.B.C. when Sir John Franklin, on his expedition of 1825-27, mistakenly turned up the Peel, thinking it a branch of the Mackenzie. Finding that it was another river altogether he named it Peel's River, after Sir Robert Peel who later became Prime Minister of England. His report prompted Governor Simpson to further explore this valley that was supposed to be rich in furs. In 1839 John Bell was sent on an exploratory trip up the Peel, but actually only ascended it to the Snake, missing the hard turn of the Peel and following the Snake to its headwaters. In 1840 a post was established 16 km above the Rat River and was known as Peel's River Post. Not until about 1898 did the name Fort McPherson come into use. Many years later surveyor Ogilvie, returning from his survey of the U.S.A.-Yukon border, headed overland and found the head of a river that he thought would take him to the Peel and eventually the fort. The Indians however warned him that "we would all be killed if we attempted it, as there were terrible canyons on it, which would destroy us and everything we had; in fact, we would never be heard of again...". So Ogilvie turned north to the Porcupine. The river though was named for him. In fact, the Ogilvie is the upstream portion of the Peel.

Unlike most of the other rivers explored in this book, the Ogilvie-Peel does not flow into the Yukon River. Rather, it flows north, through the mountains, to enter the Mackenzie Delta about 160 km from the Arctic Ocean. During its course it drains the eastern slopes of the Richardson Mountains and the northern slopes of the Ogilvie and Wernecke Mountains.

Water levels are critical to the running of this river. Low water will mean many short portages and lining particularly on the Ogilvie. Highwater will form large volumes of water, particularly on the Peel, below the Hart River. Where the river is wide there will be a choice of routes through the rapids, but in most cases considerable maneuvering will be necessary to avoid rocks and ledges. In places high water volumes cause boils, surges and whirlpools. The Peel is also subject to the raising of water levels by 1 or 2 metres over a few hours if rain should occur in the mountains. Care should be taken in selecting high campsites.

These varying water levels make grading and descriptions of the river difficult and often inaccurate. Canoeists should therefore be prepared for extra portages or lining and lots of fast, heavy water.

Wildlife along the route will include caribou and Dall sheep in the mountains, particularly near the beginning of the route, as well as moose, black and grizzly bear, wolf, beaver, muskrat and smaller mammals along the river and delta. Ducks, ptarmigan, eagles, hawks, owls and shorebirds will likely be seen as well. Vegetation is rather typically black and white spruce, balsam poplar, aspen, larch, alder, willow and shrubs such as Labrador tea. On the delta vast areas of potholes and muskeg are typical.

Access to the Ogilvie river is from the new Dempster Highway that will eventually connect Dawson City with Inuvik. At Mile 123 a bridge spans the river, allowing easy access. North of this point the river follows the highway for approximately 55 km. To avoid some of the shallow spots in the Ogilvie, and a couple of small rapids at 24 and 32 km, a more northerly put-in would be adviseable. After the river leaves the Ogilvie Mountains at 32 km the river is easier to paddle.

The rapids at 24 and 32 km may be canoeable at high water. Otherwise lining, and in the case of the second set, a short portage, may be necessary. Scout these well ahead if running this section of river. The river in this area is shallow and moves at a speed of 4 to 7 km/h. After the river leaves the mountains, and then turns east away from the highway, it enters the Porcupine Plateau. Here there are low rolling hills, covered with thick vegetation. The velocity slows somewhat in the plateau area, with the river sometimes braiding between islands and gravel bars.

Where the Blackstone flows into the Ogilvie, at 106 km, the river becomes the Peel, with double the volume of water. From here to the Hart River confluence the country is generally low and rolling, and the river is characterized by boils and surges in an island blocked channel. No navigational problems occur until near the Hart River. Sixteen km upstream from there the river narrows and several rough spots should be scouted. There are some standing waves and ledge rapids, but usually a chute will allow them to be run. 1.5 km from the mouth of the Hart is a tricky spot with haystacks. High water may make this particularly difficult. Below here the Hart flows in from the right and south.

Below the confluence of the Peel and Hart the river increases in width to an average of 120 metres and gradually cuts deeper into the Porcupine Plateau. This cutting action has created several ledge rapids, and a 32 km canyon where the river has breached the Richardson Mountains. The first of the ledge rapids occurs about 5 km downstream of the Hart. These can be run in various ways depending on water levels, or lined, or portaged. If in doubt - portage.

Approximately 10 km below the Hart the river narrows for about 3 km. This funnelling creates whitewater for the length of the section. Again, the best side and route will depend on water levels. Look for chutes or side channels that will make running easier. It will be a help if you have done a considerable amount of lining and are familiar with different methods. Below the last set of rapids Canyon Creek flows in on the left. A cabin is hidden on the shore of this creek, behind a stand of spruce.

Another ledge rapid is found 8 km downstream of Canyon Creek. A portage is easiest along the left. After this, stay on the right to avoid whitewater above Aberdeen Falls. Some lining will be necessary.

Aberdeen Falls, actually more of a cascade, is formed as the river channel constricts to 50 metres. The canyon and falls continue for 5 km, and necessitate a long portage along the right. There is a climb and walking is difficult for there is no definite trail. A hill, the only one seen, marks the end of the carry. The river curves around this hill, making a bend where canoes may be launched again. A longer carry, above the Falls, may be necessary in lower water conditions.

Beyond the portage the river widens, with easy paddling. The only exceptions are some grade 2 rapids just upstream of the Wind River. They are easily passed.

From the Wind River to the Bonnet Plume the Peel is wide and braided, with many bars and islands, a completely different river than the previous section. Like the Wind River, the Bonnet Plume flows in on the right side, from the mountains far to the south.

Below the mouth of the Bonnet Plume there is one final narrowing of the river and a few rapids. This lower canyon of the Peel has some large swells as the river constricts from 150 metres to 50. The 3 km canyon has 100 metres of rough water, with back eddies and some whirlpools. These may be very difficult in an open canoe and should be scouted with care. The canyon walls, composed of black slate are 75 to 150 metres high, with small streams splashing down the faces.

This is the last difficult water on the Peel. From here to Fort McPherson there are no rapids, although care must be taken in large volume flows to watch for eddies and boils or surges. These may be particularly evident around the mouth of the Snake River. Here the speed of the water and the 200 metre walls give an overwhelming appearance to the river. At the Snake River the Peel turns and heads north, with a corresponding change in the river and valley characteristics.

Gradually the valley and river walls lessen, opening up the vistas of the surrounding country. Islands decrease in number, but abandoned camps of oil crews, fishermen and trappers become more numerous. Soon the river is 300 metres wide with only low valley walls on the left and some low mountain relief on the left. High winds may be a problem as the current slows for the final miles to Fort McPherson. There are many interesting places to stop or camp along the river, and many small tributary streams flowing in on both sides.

Finally the buildings of Fort McPherson will be seen on the right bank. As with most northern river communities, like Fort Liard, this settlement is due for some drastic changes with the coming of the road. At present there is the native village and a white community consisting of the R.C.M.P., nurse and hospital, post office, H.B.C. store, with beads and trinkets as well as supplies, a school and a few stores. Check with the R.C.M.P. for a suitable and safe place to camp.

Float planes can land here, but it is expensive. A less expensive route is to keep paddling through the Mackenzie Delta to Inuvik, where there are regular flights to the south.

Fort McPherson is at an elevation of 15 metres, and Inuvik almost sea level. It's distance is 190 km, so this is almost like lake paddling, with very little river current to help, in fact less than 1 km/h. A good topo sheet will be needed to find your way from Fort McPherson to Inuvik. The easiest way is to canoe up the Mackenzie for 22 km and then cross the river, to the east channel, which leads to Inuvik. Allow five days for paddling, and an extra three for heavy winds that may delay you.

At Inuvik check again with R.C.M.P. for accommodation or camping, and to check out with them. Remember accommodation and supplies are very expensive in these northern communities.

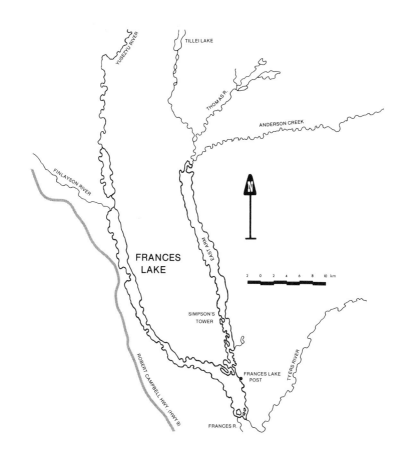

ROUTE - FRANCES LAKE AND HEADWATERS
GRADE - *Lake and ungraded river*
LENGTH - *Frances Lake - total canoeable one-way 87 km; Yusezyu River - 40 km; Thomas River - 25 km; Anderson Creek - 35 km*
WIDTH - *Frances Lake 1 to 3 km*
VERTICAL DROP - *n/a; elevation 775 metres*
TIME TO ALLOW - *1 day to 1 week*
NEAREST EMERGENCY COMMUNICATION - *Watson Lake, 172 km south on Highway 9, and Ross River, 182 km north on Highway 9*
AMPING - ACCOMMODATION - *Yukon Government campsite on* ˜*rances Lake at Mile 107 from Alaska Highway; unorganized on rest of* *ute*
1APS - *N.T.S. 1:250,000 105H Frances Lake*
AZARDS - *Wind and power boats on lake; hazards on rivers unknown*

·IRECTIONS
ut-in at campground on Frances Lake. Take-out same place.

DESCRIPTION

The purpose of this route description is to introduce those unfamiliar with the Yukon to a beautiful and historically interesting area. The rivers are not described in detail as little information was available. They are used to some degree by canoeists. All of the rivers could be approached by lining and/or paddling upstream from Frances Lake. An easier way would be to fly into their headwaters.

McPherson Lake heads the Yusezyu; Tustles Lake, the Thomas and Anderson Lake, Anderson Creek. All could be reached in a short flight from Watson Lake. The Yusezyu was used by Indians in winter and summer as an access to various trails. One ran to Pelly Lakes and another overland to the Finlayson. The lake at its head was likely named for Chief Trader Murdock McPherson, the Chief Trader of the Mackenzie district in the time of Robert Campbell. On his discovery trip of 1840 Campbell travelled up the Yusezyu in search of a good route to the Pelly River. It was August, and he wrote, "...ascending the river which is very steep and rapid, about 44 miles, and passed through McPherson's Lake which is eleven miles long, and 12 miles beyond it. The stream now became so insignificant, and that same a foaming cascade, that no craft can go beyond this."

In February of 1840 Robert Campbell had been instructed to follow the Liard river to its source and cross the height of land to discover any large river flowing westward. Accordingly he left Fort Halkett, on the Liard River at the mouth of the Smith in May of that year, heading upstream. By July he was approaching the headwaters, and on the 19th he wrote; "After ascending the stream far into the mountains, on this date we reached a beautiful sheet of water which, in honour of Lady Simpson, I called Frances Lake. About 4 miles further on, the lake divides into two branches round "Simpson's Tower" (which I named for Sir George). It is of considerable altitude - over 2000 ft. (Campbell wasn't far off. The actual height is just over 5,500, about 2000 feet above the lake). The west wing extends about 30 or 40 mls, (50 km) the East about 20 or 30, (37 km) each being on the average about a mile broad, and the water clear and deep. A river which entered the North end of the East branch I named the Thomas after Thomas Simpson. The hills slope off from the edge of the lake, along which are many picturesque coves, while the scenery in general is very striking."

Leaving some of his men on an island near the mouth of the Finlayson River, Campbell struck off west, looking for the height of land. He wrote: "we ascended the valley of a river, which enters Frances Lake nearly opposite the little Island; for the last 10 miles of its course it cuts its tortuous way, a foaming torrent through a rocky chasm. We traced it to its source in a lake 10 miles long and about 1 mile in breadth, which with the river I named Finlayson's Lake and River (after Chief Factor Duncan Finlayson). The lake is situated so near the watershed that, in high floods, its waters flow at one end down one side of the mountains, and at the other end, down the other side."

From here Campbell moved still west and north, discovering the Pelly River. Coming back they had built canoes and in them they "paddled and

drifted, hunting beaver and other game as we went along, till we reached the head of the rapids within 10 miles of Frances Lake."

"In due time we rejoined the rest of the party, who during our absence had built a rough shanty at the foot of 'Simpson's Tower' on the point of the Lake. This edifice was dignified by the name of 'Glenlyon House'."

Glenlyon House, later named Fort Frances or Frances Lake, was the first post to be built by the H.B.C. in what is now the Yukon Territories. By 1851 it had been abandoned and when George Dawson came through in 1887 there was little left. He said it was, "just above the narrow entrance to the east arm, on the edge of the bank facing westward. ....It was so overgrown with bushes and small trees, that it was discovered with difficulty. The outline of the old stockade, with bastions at the corners, is still visible, though all traces of the structure itself has disappeared."

The buildings that modern day voyageurs find at this point are from a later period of trading. Some care should be taken when proceeding through this narrow 30 metre passage as the current flowing from the East Arm is quite swift.

The Yukon government campground is on the west arm of Frances Lake, about half way up the lake. At the far end of this arm the lake narrows into a river for a short stretch and then widens again into a 7 km lake. The Yusezyu River flows in here.

For canoeists who have an historical interest in fur trade routes Frances Lake is an ideal place to spend a few days or a couple of weeks. The old portage route to Finlayson Lake can be hiked and/or canoed to Pelly Banks, the site of the Fort can be visited and the various rivers and bays can be explored. From this point the Yukon was explored and gradually developed.

Books that will help understand the area, and perhaps lead to more explorations, include *Campbell of the Yukon* by Clifford Wilson, and George Dawson's *Report on an Exploration in the Yukon District, N.W.T. and Adjacent Northern Portion of British Columbia 1887.*

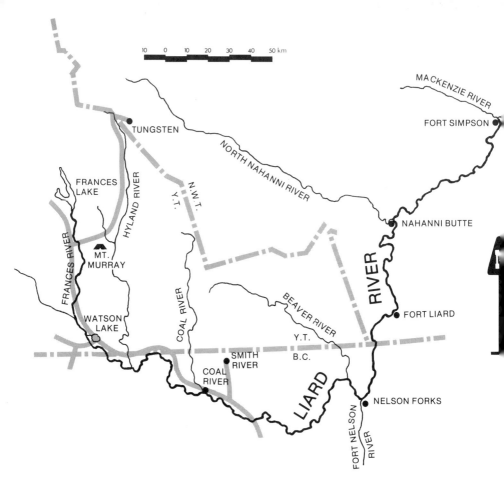

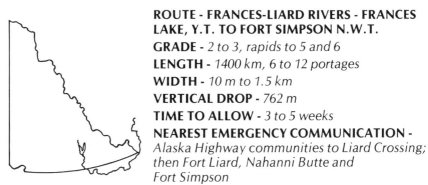

ROUTE - FRANCES-LIARD RIVERS - FRANCES LAKE, Y.T. TO FORT SIMPSON N.W.T.

GRADE - *2 to 3, rapids to 5 and 6*

LENGTH - *1400 km, 6 to 12 portages*

WIDTH - *10 m to 1.5 km*

VERTICAL DROP - *762 m*

TIME TO ALLOW - *3 to 5 weeks*

NEAREST EMERGENCY COMMUNICATION - *Alaska Highway communities to Liard Crossing; then Fort Liard, Nahanni Butte and Fort Simpson*

CAMPING - ACCOMMODATION - *Unorganized*

MAPS - *N.T.S. 1:250,000 105H Frances Lake, Y.T.; 105A Watson Lake, Y.T.; 104P McDame, B.C.; 94M Rabbit River, B.C.; 94N Toad River, B.C.; 94O Maxhamish Lake, B.C.; 95B Fort Liard, N.W.T.; 95G Sibbeston Lake, N.W.T.; Fort Simpson, N.W.T.*

HAZARDS - *Grade 5 to 6 rapids, arduous portages, remote, long journey*

DIRECTIONS

Put-in at Frances Lake, north of Watson Lake on the Alaska Highway, and one month later take-out at Fort Simpson on the Mackenzie River in the Northwest Territories.

DESCRIPTION

"Confound West Branch! It must be under a spell of malediction, a source of endless mishaps and confusion." This was Robert Campbell's description of the river that would later be named the River of Cottonwoods, the Liard.

The history of the development of the Liard and Frances Rivers as a fur trade route is a long one, filled with stories of Indian troubles, starvation, accidents and drownings. It began with the building of Fort Simpson by the Northwest Company in 1804. Gradually the posts and explorers moved upstream, building Fort Liard as a jumping off point for further exploration. In 1834 John McLeod travelled up the river from Fort Halkett, at the mouth of the Smith, to Dease River, discovering the lake of the same name, and beginning the exploration of the Stikine Country.

In 1840 Robert Campbell was instructed to follow the North or West Branch of the Liard and from its source to cross the height of land and try to discover any large river flowing westward. The search for the Yukon River had begun. After passing the Dease, then called the Nahany, Campbell wrote that, "our route up the Liard took us in serpentine curves against a swift current, through a valley well wooded with Pine and Poplar, the mountains on both sides increasing in altitude as we advanced and showing lovely slopes of bright verdure facing the South.

"After ascending the stream far into the mountains, on this date (July 19, 1840) we reached a beautiful sheet of water which, in honour of Lady Simpson, I called Frances Lake."

Here Campbell established Glenlyon House, after first finding the route and portage that lead to the Pelly River. The party then returned to Fort Halkett and spent another winter "on the verge of starvation". An occurrence not uncommon in Liard and Dease River country.

Voyageurs did not like travelling on the Liard. The route was too difficult and drownings all too common. Backbreaking, heart tearing portages caused many to request transfer to some other post or route. In 1851 Chief Trader James Anderson, in charge of the Mackenzie District wrote: "You can hardly conceive of the intense horror the men have, to go up to Frances Lake, they invariably on re-hiring endeavour to be exempted from the West Branch (the Liard, then thought to be the west branch of the Mackenzie). The number of deaths which have occurred there is Fourteen, viz.3 in connection with Dease Lake and 11 in connection with F.L. and P.B. (Frances Lake and Pelly Banks); of these last, 3 died from starvation and 8 from drownings - even instances of cannibalism are pretty well established at Pelly Banks and when we consider the dreadful sufferings many have undergone there and at F.L. we need not be surprised at the antipathy that exists towards these posts."

As the route down the Mackenzie River and over the McDougall Pass, Rat portage became established the dangerous Liard route was almost abandoned.

Later, miners heading for the placer gold of the Cassiar district struggled over the portages of the Liard to the Dease River. Since then the upper river has seen only restricted local use from river boats, and the lower river, traffic from supply barges and local river boats.

Retracing this route today requires expert paddlers, experienced in wilderness travel for extended periods. The trip is one of the most historic and interesting, but also one of the longest and most difficult. Few people have canoed the river in recent years, though there is a growing interest in its waters. Those who are interested in canoeing the Liard without making lengthy preparations should contact Adolph Teufele of Interior Canoe Outfitters in Kamloops B.C. Adolph runs expeditions down the river each summer, providing a practical way for most people to embark on such an expedition.

Before beginning on a route description a note of caution is in order. Anyone attempting the Liard should do so in low water conditions. High water occurs in mid-June and begins to slack off to the end of July, and toward September has extreme low water. During the summer levels can vary as much as 5 metres. In addition canoeists must be prepared for long and difficult portages and severe rapids. For much of the journey assistance is non-existent. This is a wilderness river and you are on your own.

Access is easiest from Frances Lake, reached by taking Yukon Highway 9, the Robert Campbell Highway, north from Watson Lake for 175 km. An alternative would by to fly from Watson Lake to Frances Lake. Access is also available from a variety of communities along the Alaska Highway. These points could also serve as egress, Lower Liard being used by those not wanting to tackle the difficult canyon section of Devil's Portage. From Lower Liard the next access point, or settlement of any kind, is Fort Liard, 300 km downstream. Usual egress is Fort Simpson on the Mackenzie River from where aircraft or road access to the outside is possible.

The Liard River, one of the major tributaries of the Mackenzie, has its headwaters high in the St. Cyr Range of the Pelly Mountains. From there it flows south and east until it is joined by the Frances River, north of the Alaska Highway near Watson Lake. The Frances River, which this canoe route follows begins in Frances Lake, the starting point of the trip.

The vegetation along the two rivers is mainly boreal forest, with alder, willow and poplar along the river and spruce, larch, pine and cottonwood in the sometimes dense forests of the bordering terrain. In spring there is an abundance of wild flowers and in late summer some good berry patches. Wildlife likely to be seen along river banks include black bears, some grizzly, moose, caribou, on occasion mountain sheep, lynx, beaver, fox, wolves, and smaller fur bearers. Bird life includes various ducks, Canada geese, gulls, jays, kingfishers, owls, hawks such as the sharp-shinned, eagles and ospreys. As well the shoreline willows will echo with the sounds of many songbirds and the sand bars will attract shorebirds like sandpipers and plovers.

From the launching point on Frances Lake there is 27 km of lake paddling, which may be impeded by headwinds. Once in the river the going is easy for the first 34 km. Often broken by small islands the channel meanders from side to side with little current.

Just upstream of Upper Canyon there are two rapids marked on topo sheets. Bedrock is exposed here and the large rocks create large standing waves. Open canoes can pass on the left side, or a portage trail can be used. It is about 1 km in length and runs along the left side. Upper Canyon is downstream 6.5 km.

The Tuchitua River flows in on the right just upstream of Upper Canyon, a 4 km stretch broken by talus slopes on both sides. Canyon walls are 20 metres in height and the channel 50 metres wide, with a strong current. There are 5 distinct rapids all of which may be run if they are scouted. The right is best for the first three and then a course left of centre, avoiding the standing waves. Three km downstream the Nahanni Range Road crosses the river.

This road, Yukon Highway 10, can be used as an access or egress point. For 26 km below the bridge there are no obstacles to paddling. Below False Canyon Creek about 2 km is False Canyon. There is no rapid except at high water. Another 32 km of easy canoeing, most of it within a kilometre of the Campbell Highway, brings canoeists to the Campbell Highway bridge.

Alaska Highway Bridge at Lower Liard.

Two km further (and one small rapid) leads to Middle Canyon with its spectacular 60 metre walls. This canyon which is broken with talus slopes is 9 km long with swift whitewater throughout. Three major rapids occur. The first is wide and is run left of centre. The second can sometimes be run, or else lined along the left shore. A portage past part of the rapid is on the left. The third can be run on the left.

Below Middle Canyon there is 78 km of easy paddling to Upper Liard and the Alaska Highway. At km 32 of this section the Frances flows into the Liard where the current speeds up to 8 km per hour and the channel widens to over 125 metres. There are many good camp sites along this stretch and some cabins.

Upper Liard is a native community located around the bridge that crosses the Liard River. This is Mile 642 of the Alaska Highway and is 11 km west of the town of Watson Lake. For 22 km below this point the river is straight and swift.

Rounding a wide right bend Liard Canyon is reached, just north of the Yukon-B.C. boundary. This 5 km canyon has 60 metre vertical walls but most of it can be easily run. Scout all rapids before entering the confines of the walls.

Ten km below the Canyon, Lower Post, B.C. is reached, on the left bank just above where the Dease River flows in from the right. The Dease is another excellent canoe route and is described in *Canoe Routes: British Columbia* by the authors of this book. Lower Post has a hotel, 2 stores, a large public school, a B.C. Forest Service station and a gas station.

For the next 50 km the river is quite braided with many gravel bars and side channels. The Hyland River is passed at the half way point of this section. Then follows a short rapid, run on the right, and 3 km further the entrance to Little Canyon. This is actually two short canyons. Scout ahead as the rapids are heavy. The left is usually best. There is 1.5 km of flat water between the two. A portage may be necessary in the second canyon as there are boils and whirlpools that make paddling tricky and dangerous. Just below the canyon is another small rapid.

Following this there is 65 km of smooth water in long straight sections broken only by some turns which create small rapids and boils.

As remote as this part of the river may seem it has been visited time and again by engineers intent on seeing a power dam built here. Near Mile 554 on the Alaska Highway there is a road that leads down to the river and several bore sites where drilling has tested for the potential of the ground to support a power dam. From the river a cable car and old spools of wire can be seen. This is known as Damsite G and has a flooding reserve "to the 2200 foot contour".

Cranberry Rapids are a major obstacle in the river. These are located 6.5 km above the mouth of the Kechika and extend for 1.5 km. These must be portaged, preferably on the left. Fireside, Mile 543, is on the bank high above the river at this point. It offers gas, food and accommodation. Just below this section are some more rapids but they can be canoed.

Mountain Portage Rapids on the Liard River.

The next major rapids are just below the mouth of the Kechika, Mountain Portage Rapids. These are similar to Cranberry Rapids and although they can be navigated in part by expert canoeists after scouting it is recommended that a portage be made along the right side. The portage is just over a kilometre in length. Rabbit River flows in from the right side and marks the end of the rapid. A sign at a small campsite on the Alaska Highway calls this Whirlpool Canyon. This is incorrect for Whirlpool is further downstream near the mouth of the Coal River.

Whirlpool Canyon, 6 km downstream, is not as awesome as the name suggests. There are some rapids, but no canyon. They can be avoided on the right.

Portage Brule Rapids begin 2 km below the Coal River confluence, named for the Coal float seen along the river banks. Over 3 km in length these should be portaged along the left shore by all but experts, and even then sections will have to be carried over. The total portage would be about 5 km. Watch for small hot springs along the portage. These rapids have huge waves and souse holes across the whole river, with rocks and steep walls to make it more interesting. The long carry is rewarded by an easy 50 km paddle to Lower Liard, and a chance for a soak and wash in Liard Hotsprings.

By this time canoeists will have been on the river over a week and with some difficult paddling and the most arduous portages still ahead the Hotsprings make a good place to take a day off. They can be reached by taking a 2 km hike from the left bank of the river, past Lower Liard Lodge, across the Highway to the Provincial Park. The lodge has a small store, cafe, lodging and service station. This is the last provisioning point or emergency communication before Fort Liard, 300 km downstream. The bridge crossing the river is Mile 497 on the Alaska Highway.

Canoeists who do not wish to paddle and portage the Grand Canyon of the Liard should take out here. It is possible to rejoin the Liard by paddling down the Fort Nelson River from Fort Nelson, Mile 300. This route is described in *Canoe Routes: British Columbia*. It may also be possible to paddle down the Toad River and join the Liard, but no report was available on this latter route.

For the next section of river it would be advisable to have more detailed maps in the 1:50,000 series. These are Mount Prudence 94 N/5 West and East. With 100 foot contour lines they show the canyon and portage routes in much better detail.

This next section of river was the one most hated and feared by Hudson's Bay men. The canyon was dangerous and the portage backbreaking hauling. When Robert Campbell crossed in 1842 it took four days to cut a trail and haul the boats across the 5 km carry.

The first rapid is begun by a narrowing of the river. It is 17 km below the bridge and 1 km above the Devil's Portage. The current is 15 km per hour and there are standing waves for about 0.5 km. Scout before running. Another short set may be run on the right. Watch for a talus slope that marks the start of the Devil's Portage.

In the days of the H.B.C. this portage was just under 5 km in length and gained 244 metres in elevation. It took Robert Campbell four days to cross. Today it is usually made in two portages with a short stretch of river between. Canoeists with the detailed maps mentioned will be able to easily see the areas to avoid. The first portage entails a climb of 200 feet and a carry of 0.8 km, across a point of land ending on a rock beach below a 1 metre ledge.

Here canoes may be launched again for a 1.5 km paddle. This may not be possible in high water. The second carry begins at another talus slope on the right side. It has an initial climb of 30 metres and then a 1.5 km carry through a recent burn. Recent canoe parties will have at least partially cleared this trail with any luck. Remember to do your share in keeping it open. Canoes are launched again where the river widens abruptly.

Remember that water levels may change all of this, and the portage may have to be altered. A 5 km carry across the whole route is easier in the long run than an upset in the canyon.

Recent reports indicate that river outfitters have cut a new and improved portage trail that crosses the ridge to reach the river at the wide point below the Devil's Gorge. This would be a safer and simpler route, though longer. It begins 17 km below Liard bridge, above the first rapid.

The only person known to have succesfully run the canyon to date is Dan Culver, an expert whitewater rafter, who went through with an inflatable. This does not mean all inflatables would survive, or that kayaks should attempt the run. This is an extremely dangerous canyon. Dan Culver runs Whitewater Adventures out of Vancouver, B.C.

Ahead is another 50 km of canyon and extremely fast water. Once again depending on water levels, most of it should be runnable. It should be tackled in short stretches with lots of scouting. Ferdi Wenger, who has made several trips through this canyon wrote an article for Canadian Geographical Journal that should be read by anyone taking the trip. His party solved the turbulent water problem by lashing two canoes together with spruce poles, leaving about 5 decimetres between the two craft.

The next rapid after Devil's Portage is 6.5 km downstream, and should present no problem. Scout anyway. Following this there is a set of rapids, past Surrender Island, just above Moule Creek. The channel to the right is usually best.

Below Moule Creek is 16 km of fairly straight forward, but fast water, past the lingering smell of Sulphur Creek to the Rapids of the Drowned. These were named for a H.B.C. party of voyageurs who drowned here many years ago. Fortunately, with caution, they are not as bad as the name implies. Keep to the right.

Now the river narrows into an impressive canyon with highwalls. As the river bends to the left, slightly north, there is another series of rapids. These vary from very fast water to heavy turbulence, depending on water levels.

Above Hell's Gate the river becomes quiet, creating almost a false sense of well being. Some maneuvering across the channel will be needed above the gate and as it will depend on water levels it is best to scout it out yourself. At low water the Gate is best on the right of the island. Through the gate the river widens again, marking the end of the difficult canoeing. When Robert Campbell came through here in 1842 he wrote in his journal:

"July 15. The water still high which ... prevented our starting till the afternoon. Only one boat was rowed up the Hell's Gate with the best eight oars; the other was launched up the back entry and we encamped above it."

"July 16. Off early but advancing with great difficulty from the height and strength of the water, which is one sheet of white foam forcing its way in furious whirlpools between these high and perpendicular cliffs, along which a chamois itself could hardly make its way, far less dragging a boat against such tremendous current."

When Campbell passed these canyon walls it is unlikely he dreamed of them being dammed and developed as hydro-electric projects. But between Hell's Gate and the Devil's Portage there are no less than four proposed sites for dams. Damsite B, with a flooding reserve to "2000 foot contour" is located at Hell's Gate; Damsite C, flooding to the "1700 foot contour" is just above the Rapids of the Drowned; Damsite D above Moule Creek and Damsite E at the end of the portage, flooding to the "2000 foot contour". Downstream there are two more sites.

Below Hell's Gate the rock walls that line much of the river gradually decrease as the Rocky Mountains are left behind, for it is through the Rockies that the canyon is cut. The Grayling flows in from the north, then the Toad from the south and the Scatter from the north again. By now the river has widened, with more islands in the channel. As the islands increase the river

Liard River.

makes a hard turn to the right, or south, and momentarily narrows. Just below the bend is Damsite A, with a flooding reserve to "1500 foot contour." After passing a large island the Beaver River flows in from the north. This was explored by the H.B.C. as early as 1824. The mouth may not be seen behind the islands.

Here the river widens again and makes several wide bends as it picks up the Dunedin River and reaches the confluence with the Fort Nelson River, known as Nelson Forks. The Forks are actually located on the Fort Nelson River, on the right bank. Canoeists wanting to visit the few cabins that serve as caches should try to stay above the island that has formed at the confluence. However it is not a good spot for camping due to mosquitoes. Stay out on the large gravel bars.

Now the river widens again and crossing its width is like paddling a small lake. A straight course can be maintained by taking the middle of the channel, but this is not as interesting as staying close to shore to watch for bear, moose, lynx, caribou and wolves. This remote region has already been planned as a settlement area. Here there would be a large pulp mill, utilizing the vast Liard forests, and a railhead for the B.C. Railway. Power would of course come from the many proposed Liard Dams. Enjoy your time here. It may soon be gone.

Twenty km downstream from Nelson Forks, La Joli Butte is seen on the right, sometimes called Cap Joli or Pretty Hill by the voyageurs. To the B.C. Hydro and Power Authority it is affectionately known as Damsite X.

Winter is the time when this muskeg country comes alive with exploration crews searching for gas and oil. A reminder is often seen along the banks where the wide slash of a seismic trail or winter road reaches the river. Twenty km below the Butte is Francois, an old H.B.C. trading post, now marked with just the abandoned red and white buildings and two cabins. Another 17 km and canoeists leave B.C. to enter the Northwest Territories.

The Liard is now extremely wide with the channel often separated by islands as much as 3 km across. To the left Pointed Mountain and the Liard Range can be seen. Then, soon, far ahead a cluster of buildings will be noticed on the right bank, enough to quicken the stroke of any tired paddler. Flags fly here and people will come to the float as you pull in, and you will have a small idea what it is, or was, like to arrive at a wilderness outpost, for this is Fort Liard. The white settlement consists of a nurse, an R.C.M.P. constable, a Forest Ranger, H.B.C. supervisor, a priest, power plant operator and a couple of teachers.

Aircraft land on the river here and canoeists could take out here, flying back to the Yukon, Fort Nelson, or Fort Simpson. Those wanting to paddle the whole river will continue on.

From Fort Liard to Nahanni Butte there is little about the river that is remarkable. Fleet Rapids occur 56 km downstream on the east side of a large island. They are usually not even noticed.

Long before it is reached Nahanni Butte will be seen rising high above the surrounding mosquito breeding area. Here the river makes two huge meander bends, making the Butte many paddle kilometres away. Check your map and do not let its closeness trick you into thinking it can be reached in an hour or two.

Nahanni Butte settlement is on some islands at the mouth of the South Nahanni River. There are actually two settlements. One is the Indian village with a landing strip that will take up to a DC 3. Across the river channel is the trading post, once run by Dick Turner who has written two interesting books on the area. There is a small landing strip here as well. Check at Fort Liard whether the trading post is still in operation.

From Nahanni Butte to Fort Simpson is 170 km of monotonous paddling. Long straight sections resemble a lake and there is little to break the sight of river and banks bounded by muskeg. There are two sets of rapids in this section. The first are 3 km below Birch River, on either side of an Island. They are easily passed. Below 3 km the Beaverdam Rapids start, so called for a ledge which crosses the river forming a drop of about 1 metre. Above the ledge there are several kilometres of rough water but by keeping to the right there should be no problem. It will serve to break the boredom of the rest of the river. At the ledge keep right through a small chute. Now there is just 50 km of straight paddling to Fort Simpson.

Fort Simpson is on an island at the confluence of the Liard and the Mackenzie. It is located on the left bank of each river. The best take-out is at the bridge that leads into town. There is regular aircraft service here as well as bus and truck traffic. All services are available.

If you are not tired of paddling a broad river head north on the Mackenzie to Aklavik and then take the Rat portage to Bell-Porcupine system and back to the Yukon.

Remember to check out with the R.C.M.P. if this is the end of your journey.

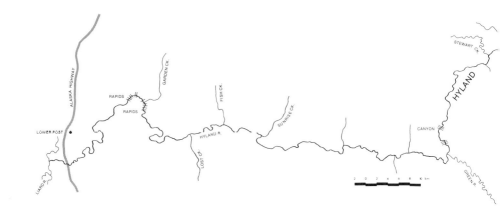

ROUTE - HYLAND RIVER
GRADE - *ungraded*
LENGTH - *250 km*
WIDTH - *n/a*
VERTICAL DROP - *Approx. 330 m*
TIME TO ALLOW - *1 week*
NEAREST EMERGENCY COMMUNICATION - *Watson Lake, Lower Post and Contact Creek on Alaska Highway near route's terminus*
CAMPING - ACCOMMODATION - *Unorganized along route. Campground at Contact Creek on Alaska Highway, and at junction of the river and highway.*
MAPS - *N.T.S. 1:250,000 105H Frances Lake; 105A Watson Lake; 104P McDame*
HAZARDS - *Uncharted route, two long canyons, remote*

DIRECTIONS

Put-in from Nahanni Range Road, which exits from Campbell Highway, where the road crosses the Hyland River. Take-out at Alaska Highway crossing.

DESCRIPTION

The Hyland River was named for Frank Hyland, a trader on the Stikine River, at least that is one story. Another says it was named for Robert Hyland, the first miner to ascend the stream. It had originally been called the MacPherson by H.B.C. people. Hyland and his party prospected the river in the 1880's but gold was not found in quantities that made it worth bringing in supplies for a seasons mining. Canoeists might be interested in taking a gold pan along and trying their luck.

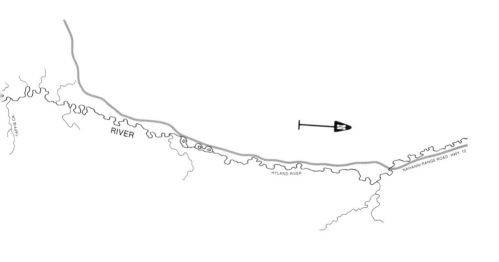

Information on this route is limited as there does not appear to have been many people using the river in recent years. However, with the exception of two stretches of rapids and canyon which can be portaged and lined, there appears to be no reason why it cannot be paddled. Warburton Pike travelled upstream on it in 1892 and found the travelling quite comfortable.

Anyone contemplating this river will have to be prepared to check it out thoroughly with good topo sheets, local information and lots of on-river scouting. Be prepared for some long portages if necessary.

From the put-in point beside the Nahanni Range Road the river twists and turns its way downstream, staying close to the road for 50 km. The first major obstacle occurs at 135 km where the river curves east around the end of an eastern mountain range that has squeezed it against the western Logan Mountains. Near the end of this curve the rapids begin, Pike did not ascend above these but described them as "a canyon several miles in length, with many rapids full of boulders, presenting a formidable impediment to navigation." Pike turned up Green River remarking that "A few miners have ascended the river some distance beyond the point at which we left the canyon, and report it easily navigable above the canyon to its source." It is likely that at least some of these rapids will have to be portaged.

At the end of Green River Canyon the Green River flows in from the left. The Indians called this the Bluewater, something obviously having been lost in the translation.

Below Green River the Hyland is "an ideal stream for canoeing - a slack current, with always good tracking on one side, fine weather, and pleasant camping places, with plenty of dry firewood...Indications of game were not wanting either - moose and bear tracks along the sand bars; beaver chopping among the willows and cottonwood. Geese, ducks, and cranes were in some numbers too, and the forest was well supplied with spruce grouse and rabbits."

At 200 km the river makes a hairpin turn to the north, then south again, heading for Garden Creek Rapids, at 215 km. Pike describes them as follows. "...there are a couple of reaches of each of a mile in length of really bad water; several ledges of bed rock stretch across the stream, causing steep overfalls; and at one corner the whole force of the current gets on to a high bluff which shoots it off in heavy confused swirls, dangerous to enter even with a big boat. We took the canoe up on the north shore, where there is an inside channel among the rocks which can be worked by a boat of light draught; but even there the current is powerful." Several stretches had to be lined, some with difficulty. Then Pike continues, "As it was with the water low in the early part of September, we had to make several portages before reaching the quiet stretch at the head of the rapids."

Pike does not give a description of his downstream journey. It should be remembered that he was an experienced wilderness traveller and a good boatman. He does not exaggerate difficulties. Travel the Hyland with care, and scouting.

Take-out where the Alaska Highway crosses the Hyland river, 35 km downstream of Garden Canyon.

Canoeing on Kluane Lake, Yukon Tourism & Information Photo.

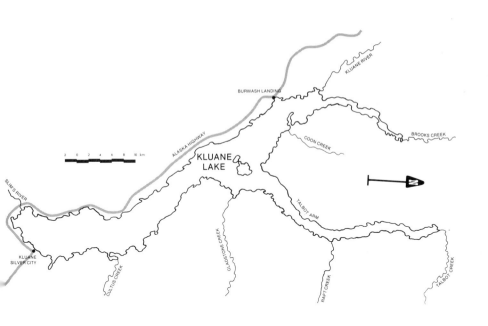

ROUTE - KLUANE LAKE
GRADE - *lake*
LENGTH - *55 km*
WIDTH - *8 km*
VERTICAL DROP - *Nil; elevation 784 m*
TIME TO ALLOW - *1 day to 1 week*
NEAREST EMERGENCY COMMUNICATION -
Burwash Landing, Destruction Bay and lakeshore resorts

CAMPING - ACCOMMODATION - *Yukon Government campgrounds at Kluane Lake, Mile 1064 on Alaska Hwy., and Burwash Flats, Mile 1105. Other private campgrounds are located on the west side of the lake*

MAPS - *N.T.S. 1:250,000 115G Kluane Lake*

HAZARDS - *Winds, some power boats*

DIRECTIONS

Launch and take-out at either of the government campgrounds.

DESCRIPTION

Kluane Lake is subject to strong winds and can be a tricky lake for canoeists, as any large lake can be. However, canoeists staying at either of the Yukon Government campgrounds on the lake may want to spend some time paddling in this beautiful Shakwak Valley.

Kluane Lake at Slim's River.

In the early days this was known at Tloo-Arny Lake, and was an important waterway and hunting ground for the local natives. Mountain goats and white Dall sheep were easily found on the mountains above, as they are today, and the river to the north lead to the Yukon, the main artery of the area.

Even early travellers though, remarked on its treacherousness. There are many shallow places in the lake which very quickly become rough water in a wind. And winds can arise quickly in this country. Destruction Bay, on the east side of the lake is a name reminding visitors of this. One story says it was named for the number of miners wrecked on the water, while another tells that a high wind blew down an army camp here during WWII road construction. Either way, it is subject to wind.

The main lake is 55 km long, with Brooks Arm to the north adding another 15 km, and Talbot Arm, running north from the east side adding 35 km. The arms, being narrow would be the best canoeing area, although caution would be advisable in crossing the lake to Talbot.

Gold was found on Kluane Lake in placer deposits and for a short time Silver City of Kluane prospered at the south end of the lake. Now it is a ghost town, marked by a few decaying cabins. In 1904-1924 there was a North West Mounted Police barracks, a roadhouse and a trading post at the site. At that time a wagon road connected Kluane Lake to Whitehorse.

Fishing is good in the lake with some of the largest lake trout in the territory being caught here. Lake trout reach 26 kg, grayling 2 kg and northern pike 15 kg.

Resorts and lodges along the highway offers a variety of services, supplies, boat rentals, gas, food and accommodation.

Pay attention to the weather on this lake, and be sure to wear life jackets. Stay close to shore, trying to avoid long crossings of the water.

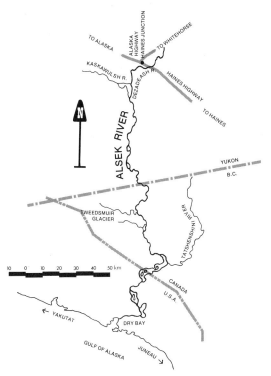

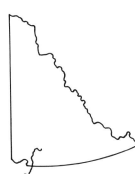

ROUTE - ALSEK RIVER
GRADE - *up to 6*
LENGTH - *225 km*
WIDTH - *varies greatly*
VERTICAL DROP - *Approx. 800 m; up to 6m/km*
TIME TO ALLOW - *2 weeks*
NEAREST EMERGENCY COMMUNICATION - *Haines Junction; Yakutat or Juneau in Gulf of Alaska; Fishermen in gulf may radio for assistance or transport*

CAMPING - ACCOMMODATION - *Unorganized*

MAPS - *N.T.S. 1:250,000 115A Dezadeash; 115 &B Mount St. Elias; 114P Tatshenshini River; 1140*

HAZARDS - *Extreme: Remote, dangerous rapids, 16 km portage, grizzlies*

DIRECTIONS

Put-in on Dezadeash River at Haines Junction and take-out at Alsek River mouth in Gulf of Alaska.

DESCRIPTION

This river is extremely hazardous and should only be attempted by expert paddlers in closed canoes who have several wilderness trips as experience.

The Alsek River has only been travelled by three known parties of boaters and the river valley visited by only a few prospectors and explorers. Anyone attempting the route should fly over it ahead of time to be sure that the 16 km portage over Tweedsmuir Glacier is passable; at last report it was not.

The route starts at Haines Junction on the Dezadeash River, although a starting point in Lake Kathleen could be used. A few kilometres downstream the Kaskawulsh River flows in from the west and from here downstream the river is known as the Alsek. From Haines Junction it is 225 km to Tweeedsmuir Glacier. This stretch of river reaches at least 11 km/h and has a drop of up to 6 m/km. Full wet suits, crash helmets and life jackets must be worn.

Below this stretch is 23 km Turnback Canyon, formed in part by the Tweedsmuir Glacier. A portage of 16 km must be made over the glacier so craft must be light and a certain amount of climbing gear, such as crampons should be included for safety. This portage must be checked out ahead of time as there is no recent report. It usually takes three days to cross with gear.

Downstream of the glacier and portage is 145 km of paddling to the sea. The river begins to widen and flows into Alsek Lake, formed by a receding glacier, and then the river flows into Dry Bay and the Gulf of Alaska. Hopefully canoeists will find fishermen here to radio for a flight out. However a wiser method would be to prearrange a flight pickup from Juneau to the south or Yakutat to the north.

Of the three known parties to boat this river two were led by Clem Rawert of Fairbanks. The first was in 1961, the first known trip into this area by boat, and the second in 1970. This later trip was written up in Alaska magazine in March 1971.

Another approach to the lower part of the river is the Tatshenshini River, the headwaters of which may be reached from the Haines Highway. It flows into the Alsek just north of the Alaska border. It was described as early as 1890 in an article by Edward J. Glave called "Our Alaska Expedition", published in Frank Leslie's Illustrated Newspaper of November 15, 1890. Attempting to reach the coast they decided to follow the valley of the Alsek (sic), now called the Tatshenshini. The first few kilometres were certainly unnavigable, but near where the Klukshu River joins they came to a small native settlement, where they saw some dugout canoes, obviously used on the river. Here they hired a canoe and guide and embarked on a wild dangerous ride to the sea, while their guide constantly told of the drownings that had taken place. Glave wrote of the trip; "...we embarked and shot out into the stream and were whirled along the raging torrent. The stream, rushing through several channels cut in the rock-strewn valley, at times is hemmed in narrower limits by the nearer approach of the rocky mountain walls which form its banks. Its forces then combine in one deep torrent which tears along at a bewildering rate, roaring as if enraged at its restricted bounds. Our little dugout, dextrously handled, plunged along the disordered surface, her sharp bow dashing through the waves, drenching us all with spray but shipping little water.

"This stream is the wildest I have ever seen; there is scarcely a one hundred yard stretch of fair water anywhere along its course. Running with an eight to ten knot current, and aggravated by rocky points, sharp bends and immense boulders, the stream is also rendered dangerous by the innumerable rapids and eddies which disturb its surface."

Somehow they reached Dry Bay intact, after passing many glaciers which calved ice blocks into the river. Once on the coast they hiked to a trading post on Yakutat Bay. There is no recent record of the river being travelled.

Canoeists should check with both Canadian and American customs before attempting the Alsek.

This route's inclusion in this guide book should not be seen as a recommendation, but rather an indication that it exists. Once again, it is for experts only.

A final note about the river valley is that it is considered by some to be the site of a lost gold mine. During the Klondike rush a prospector wandered down the river, returning with a small fortune in gold. He later took a party of backers in, and all but one of them died. This survivor told of mysterious, terrible monsters, and a river of terror. In 1946 another party tried to find the gold. They too were attacked by the "monsters" and quickly retreated. The monsters were later identified as the large grizzlies which roam the west side of the St. Elias range. Other canoe parties also saw the bears, but like the earlier prospectors, did not find the gold.

St. Elias Range.

Glossary

Air lock - Air space under an overturned canoe causing a suction which makes the canoe difficult to turn upright.

Back ferry - Move a canoe sideways while going downstream by back paddling with the canoe at an angle to the current.

Bar - Deposits of sand and rock in a creek or river, frequently near its mouth.

Beam - Width of a boat at its widest point.

Bilge - Interior of a boat below its waterline.

Blade - Flat section of a canoe paddle.

Boulder garden - Many boulders in a rapid requiring maneuvering to navigate.

Bow - Front end of a boat.

Bracket - Support for an outboard motor on a canoe.

Broach - Turn broadside to wind and waves.

Carry - A portage, where canoe and gear are carried around an obstruction or between navigable waterways; usually avoided by canoeists whenever possible!

Chute - Narrow channel between obstructions with faster water than adjacent current.

Closed canoe - Sometimes called a decked or slalom canoe, these are completely decked with cockpits fore and aft; paddlers sometimes wear spray skirts to seal cockpits; sometimes used for touring.

Deck - Small triangular section at bow and stern of canoe.

Decked canoe - Same as a closed canoe.

Draw stroke - Technique of moving a canoe sideways toward the paddle.

Eddy - A place where the current stops, or flows upstream; found along shorelines, inside of bends or behind obstructions.

Feather - To turn the paddle so that it moves through the air or water edgeways.

Ferry - To move a boat sideways across a current.

Flat water - Lake or slow water with no rapids.

Freeboard - Height of canoe above the waterline.

Freighter - Large canoe "over 18 feet in length" used to transport goods.

Gradient - The slope or drop in a river.

Grip - Top end of a canoe paddle that is shaped for holding.

Gunwale - Strips along topsides of canoe between bow and stern; prounced "gunnel", the name comes from the gun walls on early ships.

Haystack - Pile of water formed as fast moving water meets still water.

Heavy water - Large volume flow of turbulent water.

Hole - Hollow area caused by a reversal of current.

Kayak - Decked watertight craft styled after an Eskimo canoe.

Keel - Strip running from stem to stern along the bottom of a canoe.

Ledge - Ridge of rock that acts as a natural dam; difficult to see from water level.

Lee - Area of water or land sheltered from the wind.

Left bank - Left side of a river when facing downstream; the right side when facing upstream.

Lining - Using a rope to guide a canoe downstream; easier than portaging.

Open Canadian - Traditional canoe which does not have closed decking.

Painter - Rope used for holding or towing, attached to bow and or stern; the word is from the Old English panter or noose, Old French pantiere, snare, and/or Greek pantheros, catching every beast.

Poling - Moving a canoe by means of a pole; very effective in shallow water with a good bottom.

Portage - Carrying of canoe and gear around an obstruction or between navigable waterways; or the place where this is necessary.

Rapid - Swift flowing water with obstructions causing turbulence.

Reversal - Change in direction of current which turns back on itself; dangerous to get caught in.

Ribs - Curved strips of wood on a wood and canvas canoe, which run from gunwale to gunwale forming the framework of the canoe.

Riffle - Shallow rapid.

Right bank - Right side of a river when facing downstream; the left side when facing upstream.

A Dall Sheep Ram.

Scout - Check out a rapid or part of the river from shore before running it; when in doubt, scout.

Slalom - An artificial course set up for competition, usually zig-zagging through rapids.

Sleeper - Submerged rock or obstacle hidden below the surface of the water.

Smoker - Extremely violent rapid.

Souse hole - Depression downriver of an underwater obstruction; where you get soused as the water rushes over the sides of the hole!

Spray cover - Temporary fabric cover used on open canoes in white water.

Standing wave - Wave of water which stays in position as water passes through, caused when fast moving water meets still water.

Stern - Rear end of a boat; the blunt end on a V stern.

Thwart - Cross brace on a canoe running from gunwale to gunwale.

Tracking - Using a rope to tow a canoe upstream.

Tumpline - Headstrap for carrying pack or canoe so that weight is transferred to the neck muscles; difficult and tiring for novices.

Windward - Direction from which the wind is blowing.

Yoke - Wide centre thwart carved or moulded to fit over shoulders and around neck when portaging a canoe.

APPENDIX 2

The Outdoor Camera and Water

Our increased dependence on mechanical transportation for general use seems to have prompted a comparable parallel increase in the use of non-mechanical transportation for recreation. The energy crisis has made us all more aware of dwindling resources, and the need to use rapid transit and car pools in daily commuting kindles a desire to seek out the basics once again. Winter has seen a boom in cross-country skiing and summer a renewed interest in Canada's most historic method of transportation, the canoe. Coupled closely with this free energy downriver transportation has been a similar growth in the sports of kayaking and white-water rafting. Less than five years ago rafting was restricted to a few rivers like the Colorado, now it has spread to rivers all across North America.

Too often it is thought that water and cameras don't mix, and whenever a boat of any kind is approached cameras are kept safe inside a waterproof case, or left on shore. This protects the cameras of course, but photos will be disappointing. The challenge is to take photos and keep your cameras dry, in that order. With a few precautions and some advance planning both are possible.

Be sure your photo equipment is insured for all perils, so that wet, lost or stolen it will be covered. Some policies only protect against theft. Secondly you should have a strong waterproof case for film and extra equipment storage. The least expensive yet most indestructible containers are ammunition boxes, usually available from war surplus stores for a few dollars. A small one, about the size of a lunch kit, would hold two SLR's with either a few rolls of film, or an extra lens and a light meter. The largest will hold more equipment than most of us can afford. Two small ones, lined with foam and painted white to reflect heat, will make a good outfit. Test them in a tub or bucket and use them in rough water or anytime you are afraid of dunking. Canoeists can fasten one to the deck just in front of the kneeling pad. It may be left open when not in use but quickly closed. Cases should be tied to a thwart or seat with a line. Another method of waterproofing is to place cases or gadget bags in large reinforced plastic bags sold to hold canoe gear, or in war surplus de-lousing bags. However, these methods only keep cameras dry when they are not in use.

The ultimate in protection while shooting is an underwater housing, frequently awkward to use, or an underwater camera, though both of these are expensive and rather specialized. With either your problem of a wet camera is over. Otherwise it is often enough to simply lift the camera above your head when a wave approaches, or shield it under a life jacket. Another effective method is to wear the camera around your neck and keep a small plastic bag in one hand, into which the camera is dropped when the going gets rough. I have found this effective in all but the roughest water while rafting, but it is difficult to paddle with one hand. Barring all these precautions use your camera to take the best photos possible and hope that it doesn't get wet.

There may come a time when your precautions are not enough and your equipment takes a dunking. Recommended procedure is to keep the camera wet, to delay rusting, and rush it to a repair shop. If dropped in salt water rinse the camera in fresh water, then keep it wet. Either way it will have to be completely stripped and cleaned. Beware of a quote that only involves cleaning or minimal dismantling as it could mean later trouble. Should the camera not get completely soaked you will have to decide if it needs repair. Ideally it should have the same treatment as if it were dunked. If it was only splashed you may be able to do enough with a towel and a can of compressed air. It is still advisable to have it checked out. Should you be a long way from repair, and need your camera, you may be able to use it by drying thoroughly and carefully lubricating some moving parts. I once kept a movie camera operating this way for a week after it spent 20 minutes under the rapids of the Chilko River.

Exposed wet film need not be thrown out. Send it to the lab with a note explaining what happened. Sometimes it can be saved. If you can do your own processing within hours keep the film moist and carefully unroll it in the darkroom. If it will be days before processing you

can try unrolling it in the dark and drying the film, or let it dry on the spool and then soak it carefully before processing. You should be able to save at least some frames this way.

35mm, 50mm or 105mm would be a good choice for photos of accompanying canoes, or people. When shooting from shore try some wide angle shots showing the country and scenery around the waterway, and telephoto shots, ie. 300mm to 500mm for closeups of the canoes. Zoom lenses are also a good choice, mainly because equipment is vulnerable to accidents when an equipment case is open to change lenses or film.

As in any type of photography a certain amount of practice is needed before consistently good, well exposed, exciting photos are produced. You will have to learn what lenses are best, where to take an exposure reading, the most effective shutter speeds and what angles work well. If you want to shoot other canoes, kayaks or rafters scout the location ahead of time. Determine which side of the river has the sun and where canyon shadows will be. Low angles will accentuate waves, a necessity as they always appear smaller from shore, and telephotos will stack up water and canoes to make rapids seem much more ominous than with a wide angle. High angles tend to show the craft and its occupants better. Shutter speeds should be fast, 1/250th and up, to stop most action, but it would be a good idea to try some slow speeds, such as 1/30th, to impart a feeling of motion.

Canoeists who become more interested in photography should try taking a trip where someone else does most of the work, even the paddling, for photography takes skill, time and concentration, as does paddling, and it is difficult to do both at the same time and be effective.

One good place to practice white-water photography is at a kayak race where man and boat are one with the river. Scout the course ahead of time to locate various gates and anticipate action. Perhaps there is a gate that must be run in reverse, a large rock and souse hole that experts will take to save precious seconds, or a bad rapid that is sure to bring on upsets. All of these can be shot from the dry safety of shore and will be excellent practice for the time when you want to photograph on your own expedition.

Canoe-tripping and water is an ideal photographic subject and needs only a little advance planning and a few precautions to become one of the most effective means of reliving a canoe trip. For the photographer it can become one of the most exhilarating and rewarding experiences and subjects you are likely to find. So on your next canoe journey down one of these routes make a camera part of your equipment, and record the trip on your own time machine.

A Modern Prospector.

APPENDIX 3

Canoe Clubs and Rentals

Clubs

Yukon Voyageur's Canoe Club Al Omotani, Six Koidern Road, Whitehorse, Y.T.

Rentals

Adventure Yukon 510 Steele Street, Whitehorse, Y.T. (403)667-6934
Dalton Trail Inn Mile 135 (217 km), Haines Road, Haines Junction, Y.T.
Discovery Trails Box 4844, Whitehorse, Y.T. 633-5276
Gold Rush River Tours 13-303 Ogilvie Street, P.O. Box 4835, Whitehorse, Y.T. (403)667-7496
Karl's Outdoor Living Box 4643, Whitehorse, Y.T.
Wilderness Waterways John Lammers, Box 4126, Whitehorse, Y.T.
Yukon Canoe Rental 6159 6th Avenue, Whitehorse, Y.T. 667-7773

APPENDIX 4

River Tours and Outfitters

A Greenwood and A. Malloy
Box 4844
Whitehorse, Y.T.

Adventure Yukon
510 Steele Street
Whitehorse, Y.T.
667-6934

Atlin Lake Canoe Tours
Box 14
Atlin, B.C.

Canoe Arctic Inc.
Canoe Safaris in the Tundra &
    Subarctic Regions of N.W.T.
Travel Arctic
Yellowknife, N.W.T. X1A 2L9

Dawson Trail Services
Guided Canoe Trips
Jack & Ruth Small
Box 20, R.R. #1
Whitehorse, Y.T.

Discovery Trails
Box 4844
Whitehorse, Y.T.
633-5276

Gold Rush River Tours
13-303 Ogilvie Street
P.O. Box 4835
Whitehorse, Y.T. Y1A 2S3
(403)667-7496

Golden Eagle Enterprises
Riverboat Trips on the Yukon
Dave & Jeannie Martini
Box 4
Eagle, Alaska 99738

Interior Canoe Outfitters Ltd.
Guided Canoe Trip Grand Canyon
    of the Liard
751 Athabaska East
Kamloops, B.C. V2H 1C7
(604)374-9434

Kathleen River Raft Tours
W.G. Smith
Haines Junction, Y.T.

Klondike River Raft Trip
Dawson City, Y.T.
993-5391

Paul Licier
507 Alexander Street
Whitehorse, Y.T.

Thunderbird Expedition Services
Box 1819
Edmonton, Alta.
(403)424-7422

Wilderness Waterways
John Lammers
Box 4126
Whitehorse, Y.T.

Yukon Lou River Tour
Dock below S.S. Keno
Dawson City, Y.T.

Yukon Outdoor Adventures Ltd.
Box 4164
Whitehorse, Y.T.

Yukon Rafting Ltd.
Box 23
Dawson City, Y.T. Y0B 1G0
(403)993-5391

Yukon River Industries
Scheduled Boat Cruises
Box 1147
Whitehorse, Y.T.

Yukon River Industries
Yukon River Boat Excursions
Box 4001
Whitehorse, Y.T.

Yukon Wilderness Unlimited
Guided Boat Trips
P.O. Box 1126
Whitehorse, Y.T.

A 22' Freighter.

APPENDIX 5

Royal Canadian Mounted Police Detachments in the Yukon Territory

Beaver Creek Det
NCO i/c RCMP
Box 2878
Beaver Creek, Y.T. Y0B 1A0
Telephone: Local No. 5101

Carcross Summer Det
Constable in Charge
General Delivery
Carcross, Y.T. Y0B 1B0
Telephone: Local No. 4441

Carmacks Det
NCO i/c RCMP
General Delivery
Carmacks, Y.T. Y0B 1C0
Telephone: Local No. 5251

Dawson Det
NCO i/c RCMP
General Delivery
Dawson, Y.T. Y0B 1G0
Telephone: (403)993-5444

Faro Det
NCO i/c RCMP
Box 310
Faro, Y.T. Y0B 1K0
Telephone (403)994-2444

Haines Junction Det
NCO i/c RCMP
General Delivery
Haines Junction, Y.T. Y0B 1L0
Telephone (403)634-2221

Mayo Det
NCO i/c RCMP
Box 70
Mayo Y.T. Y0B 1M0
Telephone (403)996-2322

M Division GIS
NCO i/c RCMP
4100 4th Ave.
Whitehorse, Y.T. Y1A 1H5
Telephone (403)667-5576

Old Crow Det
NCO i/c RCMP
General Delivery
Old Crow, Y.T. Y0B 1S0
Telephone: Local No. 2211

Ross River Det
NCO i/c RCMP
General Delivery
Ross River, Y.T. Y0B 1S0
Telephone (403)969-2227

Teslin Det
NCO i/c RCMP
General Delivery
Teslin, Y.T. Y0A 1B0
Telephone (403)945-3441

Watson Lake Det
NCO i/c RCMP
Box 40
Watson Lake, Y.T. Y0C 1C0
Telephone: (403)536-7443

Whitehorse Det
NCO i/c RCMP
4100 4th Ave.
Whitehorse, Y.T. Y1A 1H5
Telephone (403)667-5555

BIBLIOGRAPHY

Books

Adney, Edwin Tappan & Howard I. Chapelle, **The Bark Canoes and Skin Boats of North America,** Smithsonian Institution, Washington, D.C., 1964

Alaska Magazine, **A Boater's Guide to the Upper Yukon River,** Alaska Northwest Publishing Company, Anchorage, 1975

Alaska Magazine, **The Alaska - Yukon Wild Flowers Guide,** Alaska Northwest Publishing Company, Anchorage

Alaska Magazine, **The Milepost, All-the-North Travel Guide,** Alaska Northwest Publishing Company, Anchorage, 1977

Batchelor, Bruce T., **Yukon Channel Charts,** Star Printing, Whitehorse

Berton, Pierre, **Drifting Home,** McClelland and Stewart Limited, Toronto, 1973

Cantin, Eugene, **Yukon Summer,** Chronicle Books, San Francisco, 1973

Davidson, James West and John Rugge, **The Complete Wilderness Paddler,** Alfred A. Knopf, New York, 1976

Dawson, George, **Report on an Exploration in the Yukon District, N.W.T. and Adjacent Northern Portion of British Columbia 1887**

Department of Indian Affairs and Northern Development, **Northern Survival,** Ottawa, 1972

Department of Recreation and Conservation, **British Columbia Recreational Atlas,** Department of Recreation and Conservation, Victoria

Disley, John, **Orienteering,** Stackpole Books, 1973

Downs, Art, **Paddlewheels on the Frontier,** Foremost Publishing Co. Ltd., Surrey, B.C., 1967

Fear, Gene, **Surviving the Unexpected Wilderness, Emergency,** Survival Education Association, Tacoma, Washington, 1975

Huser, Verne, **River Running,** Henry Regnery Company, Chicago, 1975

Jenkinson, Michael, **Wild Rivers of North America,** E.P. Dutton & Company, Inc., New York, 1973

Kelley, Thomas P., **Rat River Trapper,** General Publishing Co. Limited, Don Mills, Ont. 1972

Kjellstrom, Bjorn, **Be Expert with Map & Compass,** Revised, Charles Scribner & Sons, 1967

Knox, Bob and Wilma, **All About Camping in Alaska and the Yukon,** Rajo Publications Inc., Grass Valley, Calif., 1973

Lathrop, Theodore, **Hypothermia, Killer of the Unprepared,** Leon R. Greenman, 1970

Lee, Norman, **Klondike Cattle Drive,** Mitchell Press, Vancouver, 1960

Mackenzie, Alexander, **Voyages from Montreal on the River St. Laurence through the Continent of North America,** M.G. Hartig Ltd., Edmonton, 1971

Malo, John W., **Wilderness Canoeing,** Collier Books, New York, 1971

McCourt, Edward, **The Yukon and Northwest Territories,** Macmillan of Canada, Toronto, 1969

McGinnis, William, **Whitewater Rafting,** Quadrangle, The New York Times Book Co., New York, 1975

McNair, Robert E., **Basic River Canoeing,** American Camping Association, Inc., Martinsville, Indiana, 1969

Morse, Eric W., **Fur Trade Canoe Routes of Canada, Then and Now,** Queen's Printer, Ottawa, 1969

Nickels, Nick, **Canoe Canada,** Van Nostrand Reinhold Ltd., Toronto, 1976

Olson, Sigurd F., **Listening Point,** Alfred A. Knopf, New York, 1966

Paterson, T.W., **Ghost Towns of the Yukon,** Stagecoach Publishing Co. Ltd., Langley, B.C., 1977

Patterson, R.M., **The Dangerous River,** Gray's Publishing Ltd., Sidney, B.C., 1966
Trail to the Interior, William Morrow & Co. Inc., New York, 1966

Pike, Warburton, **Through the Subarctic Forest,** Arno Press, New York, 1967

Rand, A.L., **Mammals of Yukon, Canada,** National Museum of Canada, Ottawa, 1945

Riviere, Bill, **Pole, Paddle & Portage, A Complete Guide to Canoeing,** Van Nostrand Reinhold Company, New York, 1969

Satterfield, Archie, **The Yukon River Trail Guide,** Stackpole Books, Harrisburg, Pa., 1975

Service, Robert, **Songs of a Sourdough,** The Ryerson Press, Toronto, 1962

Underhill, J.E. (Ted), **Wild Berries of the Pacific Northwest,** Superior Publishing Company, Seattle, 1974

Weber, Sepp, **Wild Rivers of Alaska,** Alaska Northwest Publishing Company, Anchorage

Wickersham, James, **Old Yukon, Tales-Trails-and-Trials,** Washington Law Book Co.,
     Washington, D.C., 1938
Wilson, Clifford, **Campbell of the Yukon,** Macmillan of Canada, Toronto, 1970
Wright, Allen A., **Prelude to Bonanza, The Discovery and Exploration of the Yukon**
     Gray's Publishing Ltd., Sidney, B.C., 1976
Wright, Richard & Rochelle Wright, **Canoe Routes British Columbia,** Antonson Publishing
     Ltd., Surrey, B.C., 1977

Booklets, Pamphlets & Reports

Beware of Hypothermia, B.C. Department of Recreation and Conservation, Victoria, (free)
Canoe Alberta, A Trip Guide for Alberta's Rivers, Canoe South Book 1, Canoe South Book 2,
     Canoe Central, Canoe North Book 1, Canoe North Book 2, Travel Alberta,
     Edmonton, 1972-1973
Canoe Routes of the Voyageurs, Eric W. Morse, Quetico Foundation of Ontario and the
     Minnesota Historical Society, 1962
Four Lines of Defense Against Hypothermia, Queen's Printer, 1972 (free)
Health and Fitness, Health & Welfare, Canada (free)
Man in Cold Water, The University of Victoria, Victoria, 1975
Wilderness Survival, Government of British Columbia, Forest Service, Victoria, 1976 (free)
Wildlife Habitat - Mackenzie Valley and Northern Yukon, Canadian Wildlife Service,
     Ottawa, 1973
1976 Canada Water Year Book, Department of Fisheries and the Environment, Ottawa, 1977
     (free)

Articles

Malmberg, Don, **Hypothermia...Recipe for Death,** B.C. Outdoors, Cloverdale, August 1975
Morse, Eric W., **Voyageur's Highway,** Canadian Geographical Journal, May, July,
     August, 1961
Parry, David, **The Great Canadian Canoe,** B.C. Outdoors, Cloverdale, April, 1974
Satterfield, Archie, **Atlin, Taku & Ben-my-Chree,** Alaska Magazine, Anchorage, Alaska,
     June, 1974
Tero, Dick, **Running the Alsek,** Alaska Magazine, Anchorage, Alaska, March, 1971
Wenger, Ferdi, **Canoeing the Route of the Voyageurs** (Liard River), B.C. Outdoors
     Cloverdale, August-October
     Canoeing the Wild Liard River Canyon, Canadian Geographical Journal, Ottawa,
     Oct.-Nov. 1976
Wright, Richard, **Adventure Route through Northern B.C.,** B.C. Outdoors, Cloverdale,
     June 1971, **North from British Columbia,** Western Fish & Wildlife, Vancouver,
     March-May-July, 1972
Wright, Richard & Rochelle, **Historic Atlin,** B.C. Outdoors, Cloverdale, June, 1973

Canoeing Periodicals

American Whitewater, The Journal of the American Whitewater Affiliation, Concord, N.H.
Canoe, Magazine of the American Canoe Association, The Webb Company, St. Paul, Minn.
Down River, World Publications, Mountain View, California
Canews, Recreational Canoeing Association of Canoe Sport B.C., Vancouver

INDEX

ACKNOWLEDGEMENTS

As with *Canoe Routes British Columbia,* the companion volume to this guide book, there are many people who have contributed to its production by sharing their favourite routes, their knowledge and experiences with us. Thank you to those who assisted in so many ways.

We appreciate the friendly, helpful way in which our queries to the R.C.M.P. and Yukon House were answered. As well as assisting with photos for the book and providing general information on the Yukon Territory, Yukon House made available to us the Wild Rivers Survey by the Department of Indian Affairs and Northern Development, National and Historic Parks Branch, Planning Division.

Jim Boyd, Adolph Teufele and Harold Allanson made our research more interesting by relating experiences and imparting some of their knowledge of the Yukon. Don Basham of Capilano College assisted us with information on canoeing and first aid.

Special thanks go to friend Dave Tingey who not only offered his interest and support, but who assisted with the writing of several canoe routes.

Grizzly Bear Tracks along a river.

ABOUT THE AUTHORS...

Having six guide books published to date, and with contributions to numerous others, this writing/photographing team is uniquely qualified to undertake preparation of this guidebook.

Rochelle Wright, a former department head nurse at the Vancouver General Hospital, has spent much of the last few years involved in research, writing and general photography. In addition to assisting in the production of television programs, she also wrote a long standing column The Outdoor Wife, for B.C. Outdoors magazine. Her photographs have appeared in such wide ranging publications as Nature Canada, The Vancouver Sun and B.C. Government publications. She continues freelancing at present.

Richard Wright, an award winning film maker, has long been involved in the communication of ideas relating to the outdoors, photography, nature and its conservation. His photographs and articles have appeared in print often, including Reader's Digest Books, Field and Stream, B.C. Outdoors, National Wildlife, Outdoor Canada and Photo Life. In addition to photographic assignments, he is working on two forthcoming books, instructs college level courses on photography, and lectures at publication seminars.

Books by these authors are:

CARIBOO MILEPOSTS
Points of Interest Along a Famous Road

YELLOWHEAD MILEPOSTS
Route of the Overlanders
Volume 1: Winnipeg, Manitoba to Kamloops, British Columbia

YELLOWHEAD MILEPOSTS
From the Mountains to the Sea
Volume 2: Tête Jaune Cache to Prince Rupert

LOWER MAINLAND BACKROADS
Volume 1: Garibaldi to Lillooet

BRITISH COLUMBIA CROSS- COUNTRY SKI ROUTES   *(ANTONSON PUBLISHING)*

CANOE ROUTES BRITISH COLUMBIA   *(ANTONSON PUBLISHING)*

CANOE ROUTES YUKON TERRITORY   *(ANTONSON PUBLISHING)*